I0426927

Thank you for picking up my book. Your support means a lot, and I hope you find the read both enjoyable and insightful. Beyond being an author, my work extends into research and consultancy within organizational behavior and leadership. I engage with a broad spectrum of clients, from individuals to larger teams and organizations, offering guidance in leadership development.

For a deeper dive into my professional background and consulting philosophy, several websites are available. There, you'll also find my contact details. I'm eager to hear your thoughts on the book or discuss potential collaboration in leadership coaching.

Discover more about my work and other publications related to leadership and organizational behavior at my personal website, https://thomaspatrickhuber.com.

Learn about my specific approach to leadership coaching and consulting at https://elevateus.ch, the official website of my company.

Lastly, in case you want to reach out to me directly please send me an email at thomaspatrick@mac.com.

I appreciate your support in purchasing this book and look forward to connecting with you.

Wishing you an enlightening journey,

Thomas P Huber, PhD, MS ECS

Dedication

This book is dedicated to the humble leaders who have walked the path of failure yet chose resilience over surrender. To those visionaries who, despite stumbling, rose again with unwavering determination and grace. You, who have embraced your setbacks as lessons, and in doing so, have illuminated the way for others. Your failures, worn not as scars, but as badges of courage and wisdom, inspire a legacy of strength and learning. May your journeys, rich with both triumphs and trials, continue to guide us in our quest for growth, understanding, and authentic leadership.

Foreword

In 'Embracing Setbacks: A Guide for Executives on Learning from Failure,' we embark on an exploratory journey into the heart of business setbacks and the lessons they hold. This book is a treasure trove of insights, drawn from extensive research and real-life examples, designed to guide executives through the often-misunderstood landscape of failure in the professional arena.

As you turn these pages, you'll encounter stories of resilience and innovation, shedding light on the transformative power of failure. We delve into the psychological underpinnings of setbacks, unpacking how leaders can harness these experiences for personal growth and organizational advancement. The chapters are structured to provide a comprehensive understanding of failure's role in business, from analyzing individual setbacks to fostering a culture that embraces learning from mistakes.

This is not just a book about failure; it's about the journey of growth that follows. It's about understanding that the path to success is often paved with lessons learned from missteps. 'Embracing Setbacks' aims to equip you with the mindset and tools necessary to turn failures into catalysts for innovation and success.

This book is specifically crafted for executives who are partaking in executive education programs. It is tailored for leaders who are continually striving to enhance their skills, deepen their understanding of complex business dynamics, and expand their leadership abilities. Whether you are a seasoned CEO, an emerging leader, or a senior manager facing the challenges of a rapidly evolving business landscape, this guide is for you. It offers a blend of theoretical insights and practical strategies, making it an invaluable resource for executives seeking to leverage failures as opportunities for learning and growth in their professional journey.

As you navigate through these pages, we hope you find solace in the shared experiences of leaders who have faced their failures head-on and emerged stronger. This book is a testament to the unyielding spirit of leadership and a guide to thriving in an ever-evolving business landscape.

Introduction to the Importance of Learning from Failure

Welcome to "Embracing Setbacks: A Guide for Executives on Learning from Failure." This book embarks on a transformative journey into the complex world of business failures and setbacks. Designed to shift your perception of failure from a symbol of defeat to a vital learning opportunity, it equips you with the necessary insights and tools to turn these failures into steppingstones towards greater success. Our goal is to challenge and reshape your conventional understanding of setbacks, encouraging you to embrace them as essential components of growth and innovation.

This book is meticulously crafted for mid-career and executive-level professionals, anchoring on the pivotal role of setbacks in the realm of leadership and organizational advancement. This book seeks to redefine the perception of failure from being a mere obstacle to a valuable stepping stone, essential for learning and growth. It ventures beyond conventional wisdom to offer a nuanced exploration of failure's intricacies, emphasizing its inevitability and the profound learning opportunities it presents.

The book's purpose is twofold: to equip leaders with the insight to navigate failures with grace and strategic foresight and to instill a culture that values resilience and adaptability as cornerstones for success. It argues that the true test of leadership is not in avoiding failure but in harnessing its lessons to foster innovation and drive sustainable growth. By delving into psychological underpinnings, organizational behaviors, and ethical considerations, "Learning from Failure" provides a comprehensive framework for understanding and leveraging failure in a professional setting.

Central to the book's thesis is the idea that embracing failure can catalyze personal development and organizational transformation.

It proposes actionable strategies for analyzing failures, mitigating their impacts, and extracting valuable insights for future endeavors. This practical approach is enriched with real-world examples and case studies, making the concepts relatable and applicable for leaders across industries.

The expected outcomes of engaging with this book are multifaceted. Readers are encouraged to develop a resilient mindset that views failures as essential feedback mechanisms rather than setbacks. This perspective shift is anticipated to cultivate a culture of continuous improvement, where innovation is pursued with vigor and failures are seen as milestones in the journey toward excellence.

"Learning from Failure" is an indispensable resource for mid-career to executive-level professionals aiming to navigate the complexities of leadership with wisdom and strategic acumen. By offering a deep dive into the constructive role of failure in professional growth and organizational success, the book promises to transform leaders' approach to challenges, positioning them to lead with resilience, adaptability, and a forward-looking perspective.

The primary objective of this guide is to empower you, the reader, to emerge as a more resilient, adaptable, and visionary leader. We understand that the path of leadership is fraught with unexpected obstacles and apparent setbacks. However, it's the response to these challenges that defines true leadership. This book is an invitation to rethink how you perceive and respond to failure, transforming it from a source of discouragement to one of the most powerful catalysts for personal and professional development.

Throughout the pages of this book, you will find a blend of theoretical insights, real-world examples, and practical strategies. We delve into the psychology of failure, uncovering why it often evokes fear and how it can cloud judgment. By exploring various cognitive biases and emotional reactions, we provide a deeper understanding of how leaders can navigate their responses to setbacks. This understanding is crucial in transforming the approach to failure from one of avoidance and fear to one of learning and opportunity.

We explore the role of failure in fostering innovation and creativity within organizations. We bring to you captivating case studies of successful companies and leaders who have harnessed their failures as steppingstones to unprecedented success. These stories serve as both inspiration and practical guides, illustrating the transformative power of well-managed setbacks.

This book is more than just a manual; it's a manifesto for a new kind of leadership – one that acknowledges, embraces, and learns from failure. As you proceed through these pages, prepare to challenge your perceptions, broaden your understanding, and equip yourself with the tools to transform failures into opportunities for unparalleled growth and success. Welcome to a journey of redefining failure and reimagining success.

The stigma of failure in the business world often carries with it significant misconceptions and negative perceptions. Traditionally, failure is seen as a definitive end, a mark of incompetence, or a clear indication of poor judgment and decision-making. This negative perspective fosters a culture entrenched in fear, one where risk-taking is viewed with suspicion and maintaining the status quo is often the preferred course of action. Such a culture not only stifles innovation and creativity but also impedes personal and organizational growth. These widespread misconceptions about failure create an environment where learning from mistakes is undervalued, and opportunities for significant improvement and growth are lost.

The book aims to challenge and reshape these stereotypes, advocating for a new understanding of failure. We argue for a perspective that views failure not as a debilitating setback but as an essential component of the learning process and a catalyst for success. By addressing and dispelling the negative perceptions surrounding failure, we aim to foster a more open, progressive, and resilient approach within the business context.

Reframing the narrative around failure is crucial for developing a culture that encourages innovation and adaptability. When failure is no longer seen as a taboo but as an opportunity for critical analysis and redirection, organizations can harness its transformative potential. This shift in perspective is vital for leaders who wish to navigate the ever-changing business landscape successfully. It encourages a mindset where calculated risks are welcomed, and the lessons learned from setbacks are valued as much as the successes.

We provide in this work the foundation for a paradigm shift in how failure is perceived and managed in the business world. By understanding and embracing the true nature and potential of failure, leaders and organizations can unlock new pathways to innovation, resilience, and sustained success.

In today's business environment, a profound shift is occurring in how failure is perceived. Traditionally regarded as a negative outcome to be avoided, failure is now increasingly seen as an indispensable element in the journey towards growth and innovation. This evolution in mindset reflects a deeper understanding that setbacks are not merely obstacles but vital opportunities for learning, innovation, and strategic refinement.

By redefining failure as a crucial part of the learning process, leaders and organizations are fostering a culture that values experimentation and adaptability. Embracing setbacks as learning experiences is essential in the fast-paced, ever-changing business landscape. This approach encourages a culture of resilience, where learning from failures is integral to achieving long-term success and maintaining a competitive edge in the market.

This changing perspective on failure is not just a theoretical shift but a practical strategy for thriving in modern business. It represents a move away from a risk-averse mentality to one that sees value in risk-taking as a path to discovery and improvement. This approach is crucial for fostering innovation and staying ahead in a dynamic marketplace.

The book begins by exploring the reality of failure in business, delving into its definitions, contexts, and historical perspectives. This sets the stage for a deeper exploration into the psychological aspects of failure, where personal reactions, the impact of fear, and strategies for building resilience are discussed. We also examine the role of organizational culture in dealing with failure, emphasizing how a culture that embraces and learns from failure can be cultivated. It then guides readers through effective ways to analyze failures, presenting tools and techniques that can be applied in various business scenarios.

Strategic responses to failure form another crucial part of the book, focusing on how to balance strategies and manage resources after setbacks. Innovation through failures is also explored, highlighting the role of experimentation and risk-taking in fostering creativity and new solutions.

Ethical considerations and maintaining integrity post-failure are addressed, emphasizing the importance of ethical decision-making in difficult times. The book then shifts focus to personal and professional growth stemming from failures, discussing how these experiences can be balanced with career success and personal development.

The final sections of the book concentrate on creating actionable plans for executives and setting goals to learn from future failures. This includes developing personalized action plans and resources for continued learning and growth. The book concludes by summarizing its key messages and reinforcing the importance of adaptability and continuous learning in the face of business setbacks.

"Embracing Setbacks: A Guide for Executives on Learning from Failure" is specifically tailored for business executives at various stages of their careers. Whether you are a seasoned CEO, an emerging leader, or a senior manager, this book offers valuable insights and strategies to transform your approach to failure. It benefits executives by providing tools and perspectives to navigate setbacks, fostering resilience, and driving innovation within their organizations. Through this guide, executives can learn to use failure as a powerful catalyst for growth, both personally and professionally, enhancing their leadership capabilities and preparing them to tackle future challenges more effectively.

The journey that you are about to embark on through this book is one of transformation and profound insight. It transcends the traditional approach to business setbacks, taking you into a realm where these are redefined as opportunities for substantial growth and innovation. As you delve into the various chapters, you will be presented with a rich tapestry of theoretical insights, augmented by real-world examples and practical, actionable strategies.

This exploration is designed to challenge your current perceptions of failure, equipping you with new tools and perspectives essential for resilience and adaptability. You will find that each chapter progressively reshapes your understanding and approach to setbacks, transforming them from obstacles into invaluable steps towards success.

As you journey through the pages, prepare to be immersed in a learning experience that promises to redefine your approach to leadership and business challenges. This path is not just about learning to cope with setbacks but about turning them into powerful catalysts for personal and professional growth. The insights and lessons contained within are poised to transform setbacks into steppingstones, guiding you towards a more resilient, innovative, and successful future.

As you stand at the threshold of this enlightening journey, I extend a warm invitation to begin with an open mind and a willingness to learn. Embrace the insights and strategies presented, allowing them to challenge and expand your current perspectives. Approach each chapter not just as a reader, but as an active participant, ready to apply these lessons in your professional journey. This exploration is an opportunity to grow, innovate, and transform your approach to leadership and failure. Welcome to a journey of discovery and empowerment, where setbacks become pivotal stepping stones to success.

Chapter 1: The Reality of Failure in Business

This chapter aims to unravel the traditional views of failure, challenging the perception that failure is solely a negative outcome. Instead, we consider failure as an inevitable and crucial aspect of business growth and innovation. The chapter navigates through various definitions and contexts of failure, illustrating how it manifests in different business scenarios, from start-ups to established corporations.

We also delve into the historical perspectives on failure, tracing how attitudes and responses have evolved over time. This historical insight sheds light on how past experiences and cultural shifts have shaped contemporary business practices and attitudes towards failure. By exploring these changes, we aim to provide a richer, more nuanced understanding of failure's role in the business landscape.

The objective of this chapter is not just to redefine failure but to lay a foundation for the rest of the book. It sets the stage for deeper discussions on how to effectively manage, learn from, and leverage failures. By the end of this chapter, readers will have a comprehensive understanding of the complex nature of business failures. This knowledge is crucial for appreciating the discussions in subsequent chapters, where we explore strategies and insights for turning these challenging experiences into opportunities for growth and success.

Understanding failure in a business context requires a broad perspective that goes beyond just financial losses. Financial failure is often the most visible, marked by missed revenue targets or significant financial losses. However, other types of failures like operational, strategic, and innovation failures are equally significant. Operational failure occurs when internal processes or day-to-day operations fall short of achieving the company's goals. Strategic failure arises from misguided planning or incorrect assumptions about market dynamics. Innovation failure happens when new products, services, or processes fail to materialize successfully or meet market needs.

Each of these failures has a unique impact on an organization. Financial failures directly affect a company's profitability and investor confidence. Operational failures can lead to inefficiencies, impacting employee morale and customer satisfaction. Strategic failures, often the result of poor decision-making or market misinterpretation, can set a company on an erroneous path, requiring significant correction. Innovation failures, while sometimes less immediately damaging, can result in lost opportunities and decreased competitive edge in the long term.

The repercussions of these failures extend to individuals within the organization as well. For employees, encountering failure can be a source of stress and a test of resilience. It can also provide a rich learning experience, offering insights into areas needing improvement. For leaders, failures present both a challenge and an opportunity to demonstrate adaptability, reassess strategies, and steer the organization towards recovery and growth. Recognizing and categorizing failures accurately is essential for effectively managing them and transforming them into opportunities for learning and development.

The historical evolution of attitudes toward failure in business has been a journey from stigma to acceptance and even embracement. In the early stages of industrial and corporate growth, failure was seen as a blot on one's professional landscape. This perception was primarily due to the high stakes involved in business ventures, where failure often meant significant financial loss and reputational damage. However, as industries evolved, especially with the rise of the technology sector and startup culture, a significant shift in this perspective began to take shape.

Influential business leaders and entrepreneurs have significantly shifted the traditional view of failure, turning it into a cornerstone of innovation and success. Figures such as Steve Jobs and Bill Gates, who both encountered notable challenges early in their careers, later emerged as iconic successes. Their journeys exemplify how setbacks can serve as critical learning moments, propelling individuals toward monumental achievements. These leaders, among others, have openly advocated for the notion that failures are not merely obstacles but integral components of the innovation cycle.

A paradigm shift has been notably visible in the tech industry, characterized by its rapid development and inherently innovative nature. In such an environment, the occurrence of quick failures is not only common but often seen as a necessary step towards achieving breakthroughs. The tech sector's embrace of fast-paced iteration and risk-taking has further cemented the idea that experiencing and learning from failure is indispensable for growth.

This change in attitude towards failure has broader implications beyond individual success stories. It has spurred a cultural transformation within organizations, encouraging a more forgiving approach to mistakes and emphasizing the importance of resilience and adaptability. This cultural shift is crucial for fostering environments where creativity and innovation can thrive, allowing companies to navigate the uncertainties of the modern business landscape more effectively.

The public discourse around failure and success, influenced by these leaders, has helped to destigmatize setbacks in professional settings. It encourages a more open discussion about the challenges and obstacles that are part of the entrepreneurial journey. This openness not only promotes a healthier attitude towards failure but also helps in cultivating a community of learning and mutual support among professionals and entrepreneurs alike.

The narratives of leaders like Jobs and Gates, coupled with the tech industry's dynamic nature, have been pivotal in redefining failure as a fundamental element of success. This redefinition highlights the importance of persistence, learning, and continuous innovation, offering valuable lessons for current and future generations of business leaders and entrepreneurs.

This shift in perspective was further reinforced by the startup culture, where the mantra "fail fast, fail often" became a guiding principle. In this environment, rapid prototyping, iterative development, and agile methodologies encouraged taking calculated risks, viewing each failure as a learning opportunity. This approach allowed for quicker adjustments and more efficient paths to finding successful solutions. It also created a culture where the fear of failure was diminished, enabling more creativity and out-of-the-box thinking.

The historical progression towards a more balanced view of failure has significantly influenced modern business practices. Today, failure is often seen as an integral part of the entrepreneurial journey. Business schools and corporate training programs now teach the value of learning from failure, and many successful entrepreneurs openly share their failure stories as badges of honor, illustrating their resilience and capacity for growth. The journey from viewing failure as a stigma to recognizing it as an opportunity for learning and innovation illustrates a profound change in the business world. This evolution reflects a broader cultural shift towards valuing resilience, adaptability, and continuous learning, shaping our current understanding of failure as a necessary and valuable part of the business and personal growth process.

The modern view on failure, particularly in the digital and entrepreneurial era, marks a significant shift from traditional business perspectives. In this era, failure is increasingly seen not as a setback, but as an integral part of the innovation process. This shift is largely driven by the digital age's rapid pace of change and the entrepreneurial spirit's embrace of risk and experimentation.

Failure, in this context, is often viewed as a necessary step in the iterative process of finding successful solutions.

The role of failure in fostering innovation and growth cannot be overstated. In the tech industry and startup culture, where the lifecycle of products and services is fast and constantly evolving, the ability to fail quickly and learn from these failures is crucial. It enables businesses to pivot, adapt, and evolve in response to market demands and technological changes. This approach has led to groundbreaking innovations and disruptive technologies that have reshaped entire industries. The modern view of failure as a catalyst for innovation and growth is now a cornerstone in many of the most dynamic and successful business strategies.

Let's look at some real-world examples of significant business failures and subsequent recoveries. Each case study provides a detailed analysis of the contributing factors to the failures and the strategies employed for turnarounds.

Apple Inc. - Resurgence through Innovation

In the mid-1990s, Apple Inc. found itself grappling with severe financial difficulties and a rapidly eroding market share. This period was characterized by a series of unsuccessful product launches, lack of clear strategic direction, and intense internal conflicts. These challenges culminated in a crisis that threatened Apple's existence, signaling the need for a profound transformation to avert collapse.

The pivotal moment in Apple's turnaround story was the return of Steve Jobs in 1997. Jobs' comeback initiated a radical restructuring of the company's product line, operational strategies, and corporate culture. His leadership was instrumental in refocusing Apple's mission towards innovation, quality, and market-leading design aesthetics. This shift was not just about reviving the company's fortunes but redefining its place in the technology sector.

Under Jobs' guidance, Apple introduced the iPod in 2001, a product that revolutionized the music industry by offering an unprecedented combination of storage capacity, user-friendly design, and seamless integration with iTunes. This launch was not merely a product release; it was a statement of Apple's renewed emphasis on creating devices that blend functionality with stylish design, setting new standards for consumer electronics.

The introduction of the iPhone in 2007 further exemplified Apple's resurgence through innovation. The iPhone redefined smartphone technology with its touchscreen interface, internet connectivity, and a multitude of applications. It catapulted Apple into a dominant position in the mobile phone market, underscoring the company's ability to not only anticipate consumer needs but to create demand for products that consumers didn't know they needed.

Today, Apple stands as a testament to the transformative power of innovation, strategic foresight, and strong leadership. From the brink of bankruptcy, Apple has emerged as one of the world's most valuable companies, setting benchmarks for design, technology, and market strategy. This remarkable turnaround story highlights the importance of adaptability, visionary leadership, and the relentless pursuit of excellence in overcoming challenges and achieving sustained success.

LEGO - Rebuilding Success Brick by Brick

In the early 2000s, LEGO faced a critical period that nearly resulted in bankruptcy, attributed largely to its overdiversification and a weakening connection with its core audience. The company's expansive venture into areas far removed from its foundational building-block products diluted its brand identity and strained its financial resources. Recognizing the urgency of the situation, LEGO initiated a bold turnaround strategy that focused on returning to its roots and strengthening ties with its primary customer base.

The revival plan included a concentrated effort to refocus on LEGO's core product lines, those that had built the brand's reputation for creativity and quality. This strategy entailed discontinuing less successful ranges that strayed from the company's key competencies and had contributed to its financial woes. By streamlining its product offerings, LEGO aimed to recapture the essence of what had made the brand a household name.

Simultaneously, LEGO intensified its engagement with customer communities, recognizing the value of loyal fans and the insights they provided. This engagement took various forms, including collaborating with fan-created content, embracing feedback for product development, and fostering a more interactive relationship through social media and dedicated LEGO forums. Such initiatives helped rebuild trust and loyalty among its core audience, ensuring their needs and preferences guided the company's product strategies.

Operational streamlining also played a critical role in LEGO's recovery. The company undertook significant efforts to reduce costs, improve efficiency, and enhance supply chain management. These changes were essential in restoring financial health and enabling the company to invest in new opportunities without overextending itself.

Innovation within LEGO's traditional scope was another cornerstone of its turnaround. While refocusing on core products, LEGO also pushed the boundaries of creativity and educational value within its offerings. This included the introduction of new themes and sets that encouraged learning and imagination, leveraging technology with products like LEGO Mindstorms, and expanding into digital gaming and educational platforms.

Through these strategic moves, LEGO successfully navigated its way back to profitability and reestablished its brand as a leader in creative play. The company's ability to adapt, while staying true to its core values and engaging closely with its community, transformed a period of existential crisis into a powerful story of resilience and rejuvenation. This journey underscores the importance of aligning product strategy with customer values and the transformative potential of focused innovation and community engagement.

Starbucks - Brewing a Strong Comeback

In the late 2000s, Starbucks encountered significant challenges due to overexpansion, which led to a noticeable decline in the quality of the customer experience and dilution of the brand's core values. The rapid growth strategy resulted in a saturated market, with stores often cannibalizing each other's sales, and a departure from the company's original ethos of offering a personalized coffee experience. This period highlighted the pitfalls of prioritizing expansion over maintaining the high standards and unique atmosphere that had initially set Starbucks apart from its competitors.

Recognizing these issues, Starbucks embarked on a comprehensive strategy to reclaim its brand identity and strengthen its connection with customers. This involved closing underperforming locations that contributed to market oversaturation and detracted from the overall profitability and brand integrity. The closures were a strategic move to consolidate the company's presence and focus resources on stores that could deliver the highest quality experience to customers. Furthermore, Starbucks renewed its commitment to customer service and the coffee experience, emphasizing the importance of barista training, store ambiance, and product quality.

In addition to refining its operational footprint, Starbucks sought to rejuvenate its brand through innovation and diversification. This included the introduction of new products, such as specialty beverages and healthier food options, to cater to evolving consumer preferences and expand its market reach. Starbucks also ventured into new channels, such as digital payments and mobile ordering, enhancing convenience for customers and fostering a more engaging brand experience. These initiatives were part of a broader effort to not only recover from previous missteps but to lay the groundwork for sustainable growth.

The turnaround efforts proved successful, revitalizing Starbucks' brand loyalty and positioning the company for continued global expansion. By addressing the root causes of its challenges and recommitting to its core values, Starbucks was able to navigate a period of significant upheaval and emerge stronger. The company's journey underscores the importance of balancing growth with maintaining the quality and integrity of the brand experience, demonstrating that a thoughtful recalibration of strategy can lead to renewed success and deeper customer connections.

General Motors - Steering Back from the Brink

General Motors' 2009 bankruptcy filing marked a pivotal moment in industrial history, highlighting the consequences of accumulating legacy costs, maintaining a rigid corporate structure, and failing to promptly adapt to market shifts. The company's struggles were emblematic of broader issues within the auto industry, including unsustainable operational costs and a product line that lagged behind evolving consumer preferences for more fuel-efficient and environmentally friendly vehicles.

The intervention by the U.S. government, through a significant bailout, was crucial in preventing the collapse of a key player in the American economy. This lifeline allowed General Motors to undergo a comprehensive restructuring process, shedding unprofitable brands, streamlining operations, and focusing on innovation. The restructuring was not just about financial recalibration but also about cultural transformation, aimed at making GM more agile and responsive to market demands.

A significant part of the turnaround strategy was the investment in new technologies, particularly in the development of electric and hybrid vehicles. This pivot reflected a commitment to sustainability and a recognition of the shifting dynamics in the global automotive market. By aligning its product development with these trends, GM began to shed its image as a producer of outdated and inefficient vehicles.

The emphasis on more profitable and efficient vehicle models was another cornerstone of GM's strategy to return to profitability. The company streamlined its offerings, focusing on vehicles that met consumer demands for quality, fuel efficiency, and innovation. This shift not only improved GM's financial health but also enhanced its brand reputation, signaling a new era of competitiveness and relevance in the industry.

General Motors' journey from bankruptcy to profitability is a testament to the power of strategic restructuring and the importance of adapting to change. By embracing innovation, focusing on financial health, and realigning with consumer preferences, GM managed to turn around its fortunes. This story serves as a valuable lesson for other corporations facing similar existential threats, demonstrating that with the right strategies, even the most dire situations can lead to renewed success and growth.

Nintendo - Innovating to Regain the Lead

Nintendo's journey through the console market, marked by intense competition with giants like Sony and Microsoft, showcases a period of challenges exacerbated by missed technological trends and shifting consumer demands. The company initially found itself struggling to keep pace in an industry rapidly advancing towards more powerful hardware and multimedia capabilities, areas where its rivals excelled. This struggle was emblematic of a broader issue within the gaming industry, where innovation in technology and gaming experiences became paramount to capturing consumer interest.

The turning point for Nintendo came with the introduction of the Wii console. This innovative product broke away from traditional gaming paradigms by prioritizing motion control over graphical prowess, thereby appealing to a broad, untapped demographic of casual gamers. The Wii's success lay not in competing directly with the high-performance machines offered by its rivals but in offering a unique, family-friendly gaming experience that was accessible and engaging for players of all ages.

Building on the Wii's momentum, Nintendo continued its strategy of innovation with the launch of the Switch. The Switch's hybrid design, functioning as both a portable and a home console, addressed the growing demand for flexible gaming experiences. This versatility allowed Nintendo to carve out a new niche in the market, appealing to both traditional gamers and those seeking convenience and portability in their gaming experiences.

The strategic shift towards creating unique gaming experiences, rather than competing on technological advancements alone, enabled Nintendo to regain its footing in the console market. By focusing on what made its platforms distinctive and engaging, Nintendo was able to recapture the imagination of the gaming community and expand its user base beyond traditional gamers.

Nintendo's recovery and renewed success underscore the importance of understanding and adapting to consumer preferences in the highly competitive gaming industry. By embracing innovation and focusing on delivering unique gaming experiences, Nintendo not only regained market share but also reestablished itself as a major player in the gaming industry, demonstrating the value of differentiation in a market dominated by technological advancement.

Through its strategic pivot and commitment to innovation, Nintendo's resurgence serves as a compelling case study on the dynamics of the gaming industry and the continuous need for companies to adapt and innovate in response to changing market conditions. Nintendo's ability to turn its fortunes around highlights the company's resilience and underscores the critical role of innovation in achieving sustained success in the competitive landscape of the gaming industry.

In exploring the factors contributing to the failures and subsequent turnarounds of several renowned companies, a synthesized analysis reveals common themes and strategies across different industries. Apple Inc. faced a critical phase marked by internal conflicts and an inability to compete effectively, primarily due to a loss of strategic direction and innovation. The company's remarkable turnaround was spearheaded by Steve Jobs' return, which injected visionary leadership and a renewed focus on innovation, particularly in product development and user experience.

LEGO encountered a crisis stemming from overdiversification and losing touch with its core customers. Their recovery strategy centered on returning to their roots, refocusing on core products, and actively engaging with their customer community. Streamlining operations also played a crucial role in regaining their market position. For Starbucks, rapid overexpansion led to a diluted customer experience and brand value. The company's rebound was achieved through a strategic closure of underperforming stores, a renewed emphasis on the customer experience, and expanding into new product lines and markets to rejuvenate the brand.

General Motors grappled with legacy costs, a rigid corporate culture, and a failure to adapt to changing market dynamics. The turnaround involved a significant restructuring aided by government intervention, a strategic focus on innovation, and streamlining their vehicle models to focus on profitability and efficiency. Nintendo faced challenges due to technological lag and shifts in consumer preferences. Their revival was marked by embracing innovation, particularly with the introduction of unique products like the Wii and Switch and adapting to new market trends and consumer demands.

These case studies illustrate that business failures often stem from a lack of adaptability, loss of customer focus, or strategic missteps. Successful turnarounds, conversely, are characterized by strong leadership, a return to core competencies, customer re-engagement, innovation, and strategic restructuring. This analysis underscores the resilience of businesses and the transformative potential of adeptly navigating through crises.

Implementing strategies to learn from failures is crucial for businesses looking to evolve and succeed in the dynamic market landscape. This involves a multifaceted approach that combines organizational culture, leadership, continuous learning, and strategic planning.

- Fostering a Culture of Learning and Openness: Businesses should cultivate an environment where failures are not stigmatized but seen as valuable learning opportunities. Encouraging open discussions about setbacks and mistakes leads to a more transparent and learning-oriented culture. This can be facilitated through regular team meetings, retrospectives, and open forums where employees feel safe to share their experiences and insights.

- Leadership Embracing and Modeling Learning from Failures: Leaders play a pivotal role in setting the tone for how failure is perceived and handled within the organization. By openly acknowledging their own mistakes and the lessons learned from them, leaders can demonstrate vulnerability and foster a culture of trust. Leadership training programs focusing on resilience and adaptability can further embed these values within the organization.

- Implementing Structured Review Processes: After a failure, conducting a structured review or a post-mortem analysis is vital. This involves objectively analyzing what went wrong, identifying the factors that led to the failure, and deriving actionable insights. These reviews should focus on process and system improvements rather than assigning blame.

- Encouraging Experimentation and Calculated Risk-Taking: Organizations should promote an atmosphere of experimentation where calculated risks are encouraged. This can be achieved by setting up innovation labs, hackathons, or dedicated time for employees to work on new ideas. These initiatives should be structured in a way that both successes and failures contribute to the collective learning of the organization.

- Integrating Lessons into Business Strategy and Processes: The insights gained from failures should be actively integrated into business strategies and operational processes. This might involve revising risk management strategies, adjusting project management methodologies, or changing customer engagement approaches. The key is to ensure that the lessons learned lead to tangible changes in how the business operates.

- Continuous Learning and Development Programs: Investing in continuous learning and development programs can help employees and leaders stay adaptable and resilient. These programs should not only focus on skill development but also on building emotional intelligence, problem-solving skills, and resilience.

- Setting Up Feedback Loops: Establishing feedback loops within the organization can help in continuously capturing and acting upon lessons learned. This could be through regular surveys, feedback tools, or performance review systems that emphasize growth and development.

- Measuring and Celebrating Learning: Finally, it's important to measure the outcomes of learning initiatives and celebrate the successes that come from them. This can include recognizing teams or individuals who have successfully navigated failures or implemented innovative solutions.

By adopting these strategies, businesses can transform failures into steppingstones for success, fostering a resilient and adaptable organizational culture that is primed for continuous growth and innovation.

Creating a culture that accepts and learns from mistakes is paramount for any organization seeking sustainable growth and innovation. This kind of culture not only helps in navigating through failures but also fosters an environment of continuous improvement and creativity.

At the heart of such a culture lies the understanding that mistakes are inevitable and can be valuable learning experiences. When organizations shift their perspective to view failures as opportunities for growth rather than setbacks, they create a safe space for employees to take calculated risks and experiment. This openness encourages innovation, as employees feel more comfortable pushing boundaries and trying new approaches without the fear of reprisal.

Leadership plays a crucial role in cultivating this culture. Leaders who openly discuss their own mistakes and the lessons learned from them set a powerful example for their teams. This transparency fosters trust and encourages team members to do the same, leading to more open and honest communications within the organization. It also helps in building resilience, as employees learn to navigate challenges and adapt to changing circumstances.

Embedding a learning-from-mistakes ethos into the organizational framework is also vital. This involves establishing processes that systematically analyze failures to extract lessons and insights. Instead of focusing on blame, these reviews concentrate on understanding what happened, why it happened, and how similar mistakes can be avoided in the future. These insights are then used to refine strategies and processes, ensuring that the organization continuously evolves and improves.

Recognizing and celebrating these learning moments reinforces the value placed on growth and learning. By acknowledging the efforts and resilience of teams or individuals in overcoming challenges, organizations can further entrench the belief that learning from mistakes is not just accepted but appreciated.

Fostering a culture that accepts and learns from mistakes is a strategic asset for organizations. It nurtures an environment of trust, innovation, and resilience, enabling businesses to adapt to the ever-changing business landscape and emerge stronger from their challenges.

As we conclude this chapter on the importance of creating a culture that accepts and learns from mistakes, it's crucial to reflect on the journey we've embarked upon from the very beginning of this book. Starting with Chapter 1, "The Reality of Failure in Business," we set out to redefine the traditional views of failure, challenging the notion that it is solely a negative outcome. We recognized failure as an inevitable and crucial aspect of business growth and innovation, exploring various definitions and contexts in which it manifests, from startups to established corporations.

This journey took us through the historical evolution of attitudes towards failure, showing how past experiences and cultural shifts have shaped contemporary business practices. We saw how financial, operational, strategic, and innovation failures, each with their unique impacts, have tested and built the resilience of organizations and individuals alike.

We then moved on to explore real-world examples of significant business failures and their recoveries, analyzing companies like Apple, LEGO, Starbucks, General Motors, and Nintendo. These case studies illustrated the common themes of adaptability, strong leadership, customer re-engagement, innovation, and strategic restructuring as key to successful turnarounds.

Building upon this understanding, we delved into the practical strategies businesses can implement to learn from failures. This involved creating a culture of openness, fostering leadership that models learning from failures, implementing structured review processes, encouraging experimentation, integrating lessons into business strategies, and setting up continuous learning and development programs.

As we transition to the next chapter, we will explore the psychological aspects of failure in business. This deep dive will take us deeper into the individual and collective psyche of organizations, examining how failures impact the mindset, motivation, and behavior of those involved. Understanding these psychological dimensions is essential to comprehensively grasp how businesses can not only recover from failures but also harness them as catalysts for growth and innovation.

The journey from viewing failure as a stigma to recognizing it as an opportunity for learning and innovation has been profound. It reflects a broader cultural shift towards valuing resilience, adaptability, and continuous learning. As we move forward, we aim to deepen this understanding, exploring how the psychological interplay of failure influences business strategies and personal growth.

Chapter 2: Psychological Aspects of Failure

In this chapter, we delve into the psychological aspects of failure, a vital yet often overlooked dimension in the business world. Understanding the psychological implications of setbacks is crucial for developing strategies to effectively manage and learn from them. This chapter aims to explore the intricate ways in which our minds respond to failure, the impact of these responses on our professional and personal growth, and the strategies to mitigate negative impacts while harnessing positive outcomes.

We begin by examining the role of the ego in personal reactions to failure. The ego, often a driving force behind our professional endeavor's, can significantly influence how we perceive and react to setbacks. Through case studies, we will explore various personal responses to business failures and how they shape subsequent actions and decisions.

The discussion then shifts to the concept of mindset, particularly the transition from a fixed to a growth mindset post-failure. This section will delve into how altering perceptions of failure can lead to more resilient and adaptable approaches in business and personal endeavors. Techniques for facilitating this mindset shift will also be discussed, providing practical guidance for embracing a more flexible and growth-oriented outlook.

Understanding the fear of failure is another critical aspect of this chapter. We will analyze the roots of this fear, its impacts on decision-making and risk-taking, and the psychological theories that explain this phenomenon. This understanding is key to developing strategies to manage and reduce the fear of failure.

We then move on to strategies for overcoming the fear of failure. This section will offer practical advice and real-life examples of how individuals and organizations have successfully navigated and mitigated this fear. These strategies are designed to empower readers to approach failure with a more constructive and less fearful mindset.

The chapter will also introduce theoretical frameworks for developing resilience, a key attribute in the face of failure. By examining various psychological theories and case studies of resilience in business leadership, we aim to provide a deeper understanding of this critical skill. Practical application of resilience strategies will follow, offering exercises and techniques to develop this vital quality. Tips from industry experts and interactive activities for building resilience will be presented, along with guidelines for incorporating these exercises into daily routines.

We will summarize the key psychological strategies for dealing with failure and provide a preview of the next chapter's focus. Through this exploration, readers will gain a comprehensive understanding of the psychological dynamics of failure and how to leverage these insights for personal and professional growth. In understanding how individuals respond to failure, it's imperative to consider the role of the ego. The ego, which forms a significant part of our self-identity and self-esteem, deeply influences our reactions to setbacks and failures.

The ego is inherently tied to how we perceive success and failure. For many, success is a validation of self-worth, while failure can be seen as a personal diminishment. This perspective often leads to an aversion to failure, as it threatens the ego and the constructed sense of self. When failure is encountered, the ego-driven response can vary widely among individuals, ranging from denial and defensiveness to introspection and growth.

A common ego-driven reaction to failure is denial. In this state, individuals may refuse to acknowledge a failure or its severity, often to protect their self-esteem. This denial can manifest in various ways, such as shifting blame onto external factors or other individuals, rationalizing the failure, or even downplaying its consequences. While this might offer short-term emotional protection, it hinders the ability to learn from the experience and grow.

Another reaction influenced by the ego is defensiveness. When failures are perceived as personal attacks on one's abilities or character, the natural response is to become defensive. This defensiveness can stifle open communication and constructive feedback, which are crucial for understanding and overcoming failure.

On the flip side, a healthier ego-driven response to failure is introspection. Individuals with a more balanced view of their ego tend to use failure as an opportunity for self-reflection. They are more likely to analyze their actions, understand their mistakes, and identify areas for improvement. This introspective approach fosters personal growth and development, turning failure into a stepping stone for future success.

The key to managing ego-driven reactions to failure lies in cultivating self-awareness and a balanced perspective of self-worth. Recognizing that failure does not define one's entire identity or capabilities is crucial. It involves separating one's intrinsic value from external successes or failures. By doing so, individuals can approach setbacks with a mindset geared towards learning and growth rather than self-protection.

Case studies of personal responses to business setbacks further illuminate the complexities of the ego's role in dealing with failure. These real-life examples demonstrate how different individuals navigate the interplay between ego, failure, and personal growth. By examining these cases, we gain insights into the strategies that can mitigate negative ego-driven responses while fostering a more constructive and resilient approach to setbacks.

The ego significantly influences our reactions to failure, often dictating whether we approach these experiences defensively or as opportunities for growth. By understanding and managing the ego's role, individuals and organizations can cultivate a more resilient, adaptable, and ultimately successful approach to the inevitable setbacks they encounter in the business world.

Case Study 1: The Tech Entrepreneur's Response to a Failed Startup

John, a tech entrepreneur, experienced the collapse of his first startup. Initially, John's ego led him to blame external market conditions and team members for the failure. However, upon reflection, he realized the importance of acknowledging his own mistakes in strategic planning and leadership. John's journey from denial to introspection showcases how a balanced ego can transform failure into a learning opportunity. He applied these lessons in his next venture, which became highly successful, emphasizing the role of self-awareness and adaptability in overcoming setbacks.

Case Study 2: The Executive's Defense Mechanism in a Merger Failure

Sarah, a high-ranking executive in a multinational corporation, faced a major setback when a strategic merger she spearheaded failed. Initially, she responded with defensiveness, unwilling to accept any personal responsibility. This reaction strained relationships with her team and superiors. Over time, Sarah learned to view the failure as a growth opportunity, leading her to embrace a more collaborative and open-minded approach in future projects. This shift highlights the importance of moving beyond defensiveness to rebuild professional relationships and credibility.

Case Study 3: The Small Business Owner's Resilience after a Market Shift

Alex, a small business owner, encountered significant financial loss due to a sudden shift in market trends. Rather than succumbing to the blow to his ego, Alex chose to view this as a chance to pivot his business model. His resilience and willingness to adapt led to the development of new, more relevant products, ultimately saving his business. This case illustrates the power of resilience and the importance of separating personal identity from business outcomes.

Case Study 4: The Corporate Leader's Denial in Product Failure

Melissa, a senior leader in a consumer goods company, faced a product launch that resulted in failure. Her initial reaction was one of denial, attributing the failure to external factors like market conditions and poor timing. This denial delayed critical analysis and response to the issues. Eventually, Melissa recognized the need for honest evaluation, leading to significant product improvements and better market strategies. This case study underscores the dangers of denial and the benefits of embracing honest self-assessment.

Case Study 5: The Innovator's Growth Mindset in Face of Rejection

David, an innovator in a tech company, experienced repeated rejections of his ideas by the leadership team. Instead of viewing these rejections as personal failures, David used them to refine his proposals and build his skills. His growth mindset and persistence eventually led to the acceptance and successful implementation of one of his ideas, demonstrating the value of resilience and continuous improvement in the face of rejection.

These case studies provide diverse perspectives on how individuals respond to business setbacks, influenced by their ego and mindset. They highlight the transition from initial ego-driven reactions like denial and defensiveness to more constructive responses such as introspection, resilience, and a growth mindset. These stories underscore the importance of self-awareness, adaptability, and continuous learning in turning business failures into opportunities for personal and professional development.

The concept of mindset, particularly in the context of responding to failures, is pivotal in determining how individuals and organizations bounce back and learn from setbacks. Central to this discussion is the distinction between a fixed mindset and a growth mindset, as popularized by psychologist Carol Dweck. This shift in mindset post-failure can significantly influence the trajectory of personal and professional development.

Understanding Fixed vs. Growth Mindset

In a fixed mindset, individuals perceive their abilities and intelligence as static traits that cannot be significantly developed. Failure, in this view, is seen as a direct reflection of one's capabilities, creating a fear of failure and a tendency to avoid challenges. This mindset leads to a belief that effort is fruitless if success is not guaranteed, resulting in a reluctance to learn from mistakes or pursue personal growth.

Conversely, a growth mindset is characterized by the belief that abilities and intelligence can be developed through dedication and hard work. Failures are seen not as evidence of unintelligence or inability but as opportunities for growth and learning. This perspective fosters a love for learning, resilience in the face of setbacks, and a willingness to embrace challenges as a means to develop skills and knowledge.

The Shift from Fixed to Growth Mindset Post-Failure

The transition from a fixed to a growth mindset post-failure is a transformative process that opens up numerous possibilities for personal and professional advancement. This shift involves several key changes in perception and approach:

1. Reframing Failure: Instead of viewing failure as a negative reflection of one's abilities, it is seen as a stepping stone towards improvement. This reframing helps in reducing the fear and stigma associated with failure.
2. Embracing Challenges: A growth mindset encourages individuals to see challenges as opportunities to learn and improve, rather than threats to their ego or self-esteem.

3. Persistence in the Face of Setbacks: With a growth mindset, setbacks become a part of the learning curve. Persistence and resilience become vital traits, as failures are not endpoints but part of the journey towards success.

4. Valuing Effort: There is a recognition that effort and dedication are key to mastery and success. Effort is seen as a path to mastery, rather than a futile exercise.

5. Learning from Criticism: Constructive criticism is welcomed as it provides insights and guidance on areas needing improvement, rather than being viewed as a personal attack.

6. Inspired by Others' Success: Instead of feeling threatened by others' success, individuals with a growth mindset find inspiration and lessons in the success stories of others.

Techniques for Altering Perceptions of Failure

Altering one's perception of failure to foster a growth mindset involves several practical techniques:

- Mindfulness and Self-Reflection: Regularly practicing mindfulness and engaging in self-reflection can help individuals recognize their fixed mindset tendencies and consciously shift towards a growth-oriented approach.

- Setting Learning Goals: Focusing on setting and achieving learning goals, rather than just performance goals, helps in valuing the process of learning and growth.

- Seeking Feedback: Actively seeking and embracing feedback helps in identifying areas for improvement and reinforces the belief that abilities can be developed.

- Celebrating Effort and Progress: Recognizing and celebrating the effort and progress made, regardless of the outcome, reinforces the value of persistence and hard work.

- Modeling from Leaders and Mentors: Observing and learning from leaders and mentors who exhibit a growth mindset can provide practical examples and inspiration.

By fostering a shift from a fixed to a growth mindset, individuals and organizations can transform their approach to failure, turning setbacks into powerful catalysts for development, innovation, and success.

The fear of failure is deeply rooted in a complex interplay of personal, societal, and psychological factors, each contributing to the intensity and manifestation of this fear. Personal experiences, particularly those involving failure, are fundamental in shaping one's perception of and reaction to failure. Negative experiences, such as a failed project, a lost job, or a business venture gone awry, especially when these are public or have significant personal consequences, can embed a deep-seated fear of repeating such failures. The memory of these events can trigger anxiety and a reluctance to engage in similar situations in the future, often leading to a cautious or risk-averse attitude.

Societal and cultural norms play a critical role in shaping attitudes towards failure. In many cultures and professional environments, there is a high premium placed on success and achievement, often accompanied by a stigmatization of failure. This cultural backdrop can amplify the fear of failure, especially in environments where there is immense pressure to succeed, such as competitive workplaces, academic institutions, or within certain community settings. The societal portrayal of success as the only acceptable outcome can lead individuals to internalize failure as a profound personal shortcoming.

The influence of early life experiences, particularly those stemming from parenting and education, cannot be overstated. Parenting styles that emphasize perfectionism, excessively criticize mistakes, or link love and approval to success can instill a fear of failure in children from a young age. Similarly, educational systems that penalize mistakes and focus solely on grades and performance, rather than learning and development, contribute to this fear. Such environments can lead to the development of perfectionist tendencies and an avoidance of situations where there is a risk of failing.

The fear of failure is also closely linked to one's self-esteem and the degree to which self-worth is tied to achievements. Individuals with lower self-esteem may find failure more daunting because it directly impacts their sense of self-worth. For those who equate their value with their achievements, failure poses a significant threat to their identity and self-perception. This connection between self-worth and success can create a debilitating fear of failure, where the stakes of every endeavor feel magnified.

The roots of the fear of failure are multifaceted, encompassing past experiences, societal pressures, early upbringing, and self-esteem issues. These factors collectively contribute to how individuals perceive and respond to the possibility of failure, often leading to a range of behaviors aimed at avoiding or mitigating perceived risks of failing. Understanding these roots is crucial for addressing and overcoming the fear of failure, allowing for a more balanced and resilient approach to challenges and setbacks.

The fear of failure exerts a profound influence on various aspects of behavior and decision-making, often leading to significant and far-reaching consequences.

- Avoidance of Risks and Challenges: Perhaps the most immediate impact of fear of failure is the tendency to shun risks and challenges. This avoidance stems from the apprehension of facing negative outcomes or criticisms. In a professional context, it might manifest as hesitance to take on new projects or leadership roles. In personal scenarios, it could mean steering clear of new experiences or opportunities for growth. This aversion to risk results in a stagnant career or personal life, as the individual misses out on potentially rewarding opportunities that come with inherent risks.

- Procrastination: A direct offshoot of the fear of failure is procrastination. Individuals often delay or avoid tasks when they are anxious about the possibility of failing. This is not just limited to significant projects or decisions but can also seep into everyday tasks and responsibilities, leading to a cycle of delay and stress. Procrastination can damage professional reputation, strain relationships, and lead to missed deadlines or opportunities.

- Stifled Creativity and Innovation: In environments where the fear of failure is prevalent, creativity and innovation often take a backseat. The reluctance to explore novel ideas or approaches stems from the concern that these might not yield successful outcomes. This cautious approach can be particularly detrimental in fields that thrive on innovation, such as technology, arts, or research, where new and untested ideas are the lifeblood of progress.

- Overly Cautious Decision-Making: Decision-making processes can become overly cautious or even paralyzed in the face of failure-related fear. The desire to avoid failure at all costs can lead to indecision, where every option seems fraught with potential pitfalls. This can result in missed deadlines, slow response times, and opportunities lost to competitors who are more willing to take calculated risks.

- Impact on Personal and Professional Growth: The fear of failure can significantly hinder personal and professional development. It creates a barrier to learning from mistakes and growing from experiences. Individuals may find themselves stuck in their comfort zones, unable to expand their skills or advance in their careers.

- Increased Stress and Anxiety: Living in constant fear of failure can take a toll on mental health, leading to increased levels of stress and anxiety. This state of chronic stress can have physical health implications as well, such as sleep disturbances, fatigue, and a weakened immune system. Moreover, it can deteriorate the quality of life, affecting relationships, job satisfaction, and overall happiness.

The fear of failure casts a wide net, influencing various aspects of life and work. Its impacts are not just limited to missed opportunities but extend to mental well-being, personal growth, creativity, and decision-making capabilities. Understanding and addressing this fear is crucial for individuals seeking to lead a balanced, productive, and fulfilling life.

Understanding the fear of failure requires delving into various psychological theories that explain its origins and manifestations. Attribution Theory, for instance, points out that this fear often arises from negative self-explanations for failing. Individuals may perceive failure as a direct reflection of their lack of ability or effort, which negatively impacts their self-esteem and motivation. This perspective can lead to a heightened fear of similar situations in the future, perpetuating a cycle of avoidance and anxiety.

Achievement Goal Theory offers another lens, suggesting that the nature of an individual's goals plays a crucial role in their fear of failure. Those who set performance goals, which are centered around demonstrating their abilities, often experience a greater fear of failure compared to those with learning goals, who are more focused on improving and developing their skills. The fear in the former arises from the possibility of not meeting the standards they've set for showcasing their abilities, leading to anxiety and stress.

Self-Efficacy Theory contributes to this understanding by focusing on an individual's belief in their ability to succeed. Those with low self-efficacy, who doubt their capabilities to achieve desired outcomes, are more likely to fear failure. This lack of confidence in their own abilities can lead to a reluctance to engage in challenging tasks or opportunities, limiting their potential for growth and learning.

Self-Worth Theory delves into the deep connection between fear of failure and personal identity. It posits that for some individuals, self-worth is intricately linked to their success. Failure, therefore, poses not just a professional or external setback, but a profound threat to their sense of self and identity. This theory underscores how deeply failure can affect an individual's psyche, particularly when success is seen as a core component of self-worth.

Cognitive-Behavioral Theories approach the fear of failure from the perspective of thought patterns and beliefs. According to these theories, negative and irrational beliefs about failure lead to fear and avoidance behaviors. The emphasis here is on how individuals process and think about failure. By identifying and altering these negative thought patterns, it is possible to manage and reduce the fear of failure, leading to healthier behaviors and attitudes.

These psychological theories collectively provide a comprehensive understanding of the fear of failure. They highlight how perceptions, beliefs, goals, and self-worth are intertwined in shaping how individuals respond to the prospect of failing. This multifaceted approach offers valuable insights for addressing and overcoming the fear of failure, suggesting that changes in thought patterns, goal setting, and self-perception can significantly mitigate its impact.

Overcoming the fear of failure is a multifaceted process that involves a combination of introspection, behavioral changes, and cognitive restructuring. It starts with acknowledging and understanding the fear, followed by developing strategies to manage and gradually reduce its influence.

One effective approach is to actively reframe the concept of failure. Instead of viewing failure as a negative endpoint, it can be seen as a valuable learning opportunity. This shift in perspective helps in reducing the stigma attached to failure and encourages a more experimental and risk-taking mindset. Emphasizing learning and growth over success and perfection can transform the way failures are perceived and handled.

Building resilience is another key strategy in overcoming this fear. Resilience involves developing a robust psychological foundation that enables individuals to bounce back from setbacks and challenges. This can be nurtured through practices like mindfulness, which promotes a non-judgmental awareness of the present moment, and resilience training, which focuses on building skills like optimism, flexibility, and problem-solving.

Developing a support system plays a crucial role in managing the fear of failure. Having a network of colleagues, mentors, or friends who provide encouragement, perspective, and honest feedback can make facing and learning from failures much easier. This support system can also provide a sense of security and belonging, mitigating the isolation and self-doubt that often accompany failures.

Setting realistic and achievable goals can also help in reducing the fear of failure. By breaking down larger goals into smaller, manageable tasks, the overwhelming pressure to succeed is diminished. This approach allows for celebrating small wins and learning from minor setbacks, thereby fostering a sense of progress and competence.

Practicing self-compassion is vital in managing the fear of failure. Being kind to oneself and recognizing that failure is a universal experience can alleviate the harsh self-judgment that often accompanies setbacks. Self-compassion involves treating oneself with the same kindness and understanding that one would offer to a friend in a similar situation.

Engaging in cognitive-behavioral techniques such as challenging negative thought patterns and beliefs about failure can also be beneficial. This might involve identifying and disputing irrational beliefs, focusing on evidence-based thinking, and developing more balanced and rational perspectives about success and failure.

Learning from successful role models who have overcome failure can provide inspiration and practical insights. Hearing their stories of setbacks and resilience can demystify the journey of overcoming failure, providing real-life examples of how failures can be steppingstones to success.

Overcoming the fear of failure is a process that requires changing how failure is perceived, building resilience, seeking support, setting achievable goals, practicing self-compassion, employing cognitive-behavioral strategies, and learning from others. These strategies collectively contribute to a healthier approach to facing and learning from failures, ultimately leading to personal and professional growth.

Overcoming the fear of failure is often best illustrated through real-life examples, where individuals or organizations have faced and conquered this challenge, transforming their approach and achieving success.

- J.K. Rowling: Before becoming one of the most successful authors of all time, J.K. Rowling faced numerous rejections for her manuscript of "Harry Potter and the Philosopher's Stone." Living as a single mother on welfare, she persevered through these rejections and her personal struggles. Her resilience and refusal to give in to the fear of failure eventually led to the publication and unprecedented success of the Harry Potter series.

- Thomas Edison: Known for inventing the light bulb, Thomas Edison's journey to success was filled with setbacks. He famously said, "I have not failed. I've just found 10,000 ways that won't work." Edison's approach to failure as a learning opportunity rather than a setback was key to his eventual success as an inventor.

- Oprah Winfrey: Before becoming a media mogul, Oprah Winfrey faced numerous career setbacks, including being fired from her job as a television reporter because she was "unfit for TV." Instead of letting this failure define her, she used it as motivation to pursue a career in television, eventually leading to the success of "The Oprah Winfrey Show."

- Steve Jobs: After co-founding Apple Inc., Steve Jobs was eventually fired from his own company. This setback didn't deter him; instead, he went on to found NeXT and Pixar, with both ventures achieving significant success. His return to

Apple marked a turning point for the company, leading to innovative products like the iPod, iPhone, and iPad.

- Airbnb: The founders of Airbnb faced numerous rejections and failures in the early days of their startup. They had difficulty securing funding and faced skepticism about their business model. However, they persisted, continuously adapting and improving their platform. Their determination paid off, and Airbnb became a revolutionary force in the hospitality industry.

- Colonel Sanders: The story of Colonel Sanders, the founder of Kentucky Fried Chicken (KFC), is a classic example of overcoming the fear of failure. He started franchising his restaurant concept at the age of 65, after facing multiple rejections and failures in his earlier career. His persistence and belief in his fried chicken recipe led to the global success of KFC.

These examples highlight the diverse ways in which individuals and organizations can overcome the fear of failure. They demonstrate that persistence, resilience, and a positive mindset in the face of setbacks can lead to remarkable achievements and success. Each story underscores the importance of viewing failure not as an insurmountable obstacle but as an integral part of the journey to success.

Developing resilience, the ability to recover and thrive in the face of challenges, is an essential skill in both personal and professional realms. Various psychological frameworks provide insights into building and strengthening this vital attribute.

One influential framework is the concept of psychological resilience, which refers to the process of adapting well in the face of adversity, trauma, tragedy, threats, or significant sources of stress. This framework suggests that resilience is not a trait that people either have or do not have, but involves behaviors, thoughts, and actions that can be learned and developed in anyone.

Another important model is the Positive Psychology approach, introduced by Martin Seligman. This framework focuses on enhancing individual strengths rather than merely repairing weaknesses. It emphasizes the development of traits like optimism, gratitude, and compassion, which are considered essential for building resilience. Positive Psychology suggests that by nurturing these positive traits, individuals can better cope with and recover from adverse experiences.

The Cognitive-Behavioral approach also offers valuable insights into developing resilience. This framework posits that our thoughts and perceptions significantly influence our emotional and behavioral responses to situations. By identifying and challenging negative thought patterns and beliefs, and replacing them with more balanced and rational ones, individuals can develop greater resilience in the face of challenges.

Another noteworthy framework is the Emotional Intelligence model, proposed by Daniel Goleman, which underscores the importance of being aware of, understanding, and managing our emotions and the emotions of others. This approach suggests that high emotional intelligence is key to developing resilience, as it enables individuals to navigate emotional challenges more effectively and maintain psychological well-being.

The concept of Mindfulness, rooted in Buddhist philosophy and adapted in psychological practice, is another framework that contributes to resilience. Mindfulness involves maintaining a moment-by-moment awareness of our thoughts, feelings, bodily sensations, and surrounding environment. This practice encourages acceptance and non-judgment, which can help individuals maintain a calm and clear perspective in difficult situations, thereby enhancing resilience.

Lastly, the Neurobiological approach provides insights into the physical and biological aspects of resilience. Research in this area explores how factors like genetics, brain chemistry, and hormonal responses influence an individual's capacity to cope with stress and adversity. Understanding these biological factors can inform strategies to bolster psychological resilience.

In summary, these psychological frameworks collectively offer a rich understanding of resilience. By integrating insights from these diverse approaches, individuals can develop a robust set of tools and strategies to enhance their resilience, enabling them to better navigate the challenges and adversities of life.

Real-life case studies of resilience in business leadership often provide some of the most compelling and instructive examples of how to overcome adversity. Here are several notable cases, distinct from the ones previously mentioned:

- Satya Nadella, Microsoft: When Satya Nadella took over as CEO in 2014, Microsoft was perceived as lagging behind its competitors. Nadella demonstrated resilience by shifting the company's focus towards cloud computing and reinventing its culture, encouraging collaboration and innovation. His leadership has been instrumental in Microsoft's renewed success and growth in new technology areas.

- Howard Schultz, Starbucks: Schultz's journey with Starbucks has been marked by resilience. After stepping down as CEO, he returned in 2008 when the company was struggling. Schultz made tough decisions, including closing stores and retraining employees, to revive the brand's customer experience. His resilience and commitment to the company's core values helped Starbucks rebound and continue as a global coffee leader.

- Indra Nooyi, PepsiCo: As the former CEO of PepsiCo, Indra Nooyi faced significant challenges in shifting the company's focus towards healthier products in response to changing consumer preferences. Her resilience in the face of skepticism and resistance was pivotal in successfully transforming PepsiCo's product line and sustaining its growth in a competitive market.

- Mary Barra, General Motors: Taking the helm of General Motors post-bankruptcy and during a massive recall crisis, Mary Barra's resilience was tested early in her tenure as CEO. She navigated the company through these challenges with a focus on transparency, accountability, and a commitment to safety and quality. Under her leadership, GM has made significant strides in rebuilding its reputation and investing in electric vehicles.

- Brian Chesky, Airbnb: As the co-founder and CEO of Airbnb, Brian Chesky faced considerable challenges during the COVID-19 pandemic when the travel industry came to a near standstill. Chesky's resilience was evident in how he quickly pivoted the company, focusing on local and long-term stays, and restructured the company to survive the downturn. His leadership during this period helped Airbnb to rebound and go public with a successful IPO.

- Vera Wang: Before becoming a renowned fashion designer, Vera Wang was a figure skater and journalist. She entered the fashion industry at the age of 40, a time when many would consider it too late to start a new career. Her resilience and dedication to her vision led to the creation of a legendary bridal wear empire.

These case studies exemplify the crucial role of resilience in business leadership. Each of these leaders faced significant challenges and setbacks but used these as opportunities for growth, learning, and reinvention. Their stories provide inspiration and lessons in resilience for current and future business leaders.

Developing resilience is a dynamic process that can be integrated into daily routines through various exercises and techniques. These practices help individuals to cope with and recover from setbacks more effectively, enhancing their ability to navigate challenges.

Reflective Journaling is a powerful tool for fostering a growth mindset. Regularly writing about daily experiences, especially challenges, and focusing on what was learned from them encourages a shift in perspective. Implementing this into a daily routine can be as simple as setting aside a few minutes each day, perhaps in the morning or before bed, to jot down thoughts and reflections.

Goal-Setting and Task Breakdown involves establishing achievable goals and breaking them down into smaller, manageable tasks. This can be integrated into daily planning. At the start of each week, outline the main goals and then each day, break these down into smaller tasks, celebrating their completion to build a sense of progress and motivation.

Incorporating Mindfulness and Meditation into everyday life enhances present-moment awareness and reduces stress. This could involve starting the day with a short meditation session or taking short mindfulness breaks throughout the day, using techniques like focused breathing or mindful observation.

Developing Problem-Solving Skills can be nurtured through engaging in activities that require creative thinking. Allocating time each week to activities like puzzles, strategy games, or even brainstorming sessions on various topics can sharpen these skills.

Participating in Resilience Workshops or Training Programs offers both theoretical knowledge and practical tools for handling adversity. Scheduling time to attend these workshops, whether in-person or online, can significantly enhance one's resilience toolkit.

Role-Playing Scenarios that simulate stressful situations help in developing adaptability. This can be practiced in safe environments like training sessions or even with friends and family, where one can role-play responses to various challenging scenarios.

Building a Social Support Network is key to resilience. This involves actively engaging in social activities, joining clubs or groups, or strengthening existing relationships. Making time for social activities in one's schedule, even if it's a virtual meetup, can provide significant emotional support.

Maintaining Physical Wellness through regular exercise is crucial for stress management. Incorporating physical activities into daily life, whether it's a morning yoga session, a lunchtime walk, or an evening workout, helps in building mental strength.

Gratitude Diaries encourage a positive outlook. Every day, take a moment to write down things you are grateful for. This practice can be coupled with morning or evening routines, serving as a reminder of the positive aspects of life.

Stress Management Techniques like progressive muscle relaxation or deep breathing exercises can be used during moments of stress or as a regular practice. Allocating a few minutes each day for these exercises can help in managing stress levels.

Decision-Making Exercises can be incorporated into regular learning sessions, perhaps as part of a weekly personal development routine. Analyzing different scenarios and exploring decision-making processes can enhance problem-solving skills.

Creating a Resilience Sharing Forum online where experiences and strategies can be shared builds a community of support. Participating in these forums can be a regular part of one's online social interactions, offering a space to both give and receive advice and encouragement.

By weaving these practices into daily routines, individuals can gradually build and strengthen their resilience, enabling them to better handle life's challenges and recover more effectively from setbacks.

In this chapter, we have explored a range of psychological strategies essential for effectively dealing with failure. The journey began with understanding the fear of failure, its roots, and its impacts on behavior and decision-making. We delved into various psychological theories that explain this fear, including Attribution Theory, Achievement Goal Theory, and Self-Efficacy Theory, among others. These theories provide a comprehensive framework for understanding how our perceptions, beliefs, and goals shape our responses to failure.

We then examined practical approaches to overcoming the fear of failure. Key among these is the development of resilience, a critical skill in the face of adversity. We discussed how resilience can be built and strengthened through reflective journaling, goal-setting, mindfulness practices, and engaging in problem-solving activities. Additionally, we highlighted the importance of a supportive social network, physical wellness, and stress management techniques in fostering a resilient mindset.

The chapter also presented interactive activities and exercises designed to integrate resilience-building practices into daily routines. These practical tools aim to empower individuals to transform their approach to challenges, encouraging a mindset that views failures as opportunities for growth and learning.

As we conclude this chapter, it's clear that the psychological strategies discussed here are pivotal in redefining our relationship with failure. By embracing these approaches, individuals can cultivate a more resilient, adaptable, and growth-oriented mindset, turning setbacks into valuable learning experiences.

In the next chapter, we will shift our focus from the individual to the organizational level, exploring how organizational culture influences the perception and handling of failure. We will examine the role of leadership, policies, and communication in creating an environment where failure is not feared but used as a catalyst for innovation and improvement.

This chapter will delve into case studies of organizations that have successfully fostered a culture of learning from failure. We will explore strategies for building a resilient organizational culture, where transparency, open communication, and continuous learning are integral. The aim is to provide leaders and managers with insights and tools to cultivate a workplace where the fear of failure does not stifle creativity and innovation but rather contributes to the overall growth and success of the organization.

Chapter 3: Organizational Culture and Failure

In Chapter 3, "Organizational Culture and Failure," we embark on an exploration of how the fabric of an organization's culture significantly influences its approach to failure. The chapter aims to unravel the complex relationship between organizational culture and the ways in which businesses perceive, respond to, and learn from failures. This exploration is critical, as the culture within an organization can either be a catalyst for growth and innovation or a barrier to progress.

At the heart of any organization lies its culture – a unique blend of values, beliefs, rituals, norms, and practices that define the way things are done. Organizational culture is the invisible force that shapes behaviors, guides decision-making, and influences the overall direction of a business. It encompasses everything from the organization's work environment, leadership styles, communication patterns, to the implicit expectations placed upon its members.

This culture plays a pivotal role in determining how failure is approached and managed within an organization. In cultures where failure is stigmatized, it often leads to risk aversion and a reluctance to innovate. Conversely, in cultures that view failure as an opportunity for learning and growth, there is a tendency to embrace risks and foster innovation.

The impact of organizational culture extends beyond immediate responses to failure. It also affects employee morale, engagement, retention, and ultimately, the organization's ability to achieve its strategic goals. A positive culture, one that constructively deals with failure, can lead to a more resilient and adaptable organization.

In the upcoming sections, we will delve deeper into the dynamics of organizational culture and its interplay with failure, exploring how leaders can shape a culture that positively engages with setbacks and challenges.

The Role of Failure in Organizational Culture is a critical aspect that warrants in-depth analysis, as it significantly influences how a company navigates challenges and pursues innovation. The perception and management of failure within an organization are deeply rooted in its culture, shaping responses to setbacks and influencing long-term success.

In organizational cultures where failure is stigmatized, there's often a pervasive fear of taking risks. In such environments, failure is viewed as a threat to one's professional standing or the company's reputation. This perception can lead to conservative decision-making, where safe and tried methods are preferred over innovative or untested solutions. The consequence is a potentially stifling environment for creativity and innovation, as employees may shy away from proposing or pursuing bold ideas due to fear of repercussions if they fail.

Conversely, cultures that embrace failure as a learning opportunity tend to foster resilience and adaptability. In these organizations, failure is not celebrated but is acknowledged as an integral part of the innovation process. Such cultures understand that setbacks are valuable experiences from which crucial lessons can be drawn. This approach encourages experimentation and calculated risk-taking, creating a dynamic environment where novel ideas are tested and refined. It's not the failure itself that's important, but the learning and improvement that come from it.

Leadership plays a pivotal role in shaping the organization's approach to failure. Leaders who openly discuss their failures and the lessons learned set a tone of transparency and humility. This attitude can trickle down through the organizational hierarchy, cultivating a culture where employees feel safe to take risks and speak openly about challenges and setbacks.

The systems and processes within an organization can either facilitate or hinder learning from failure. For instance, a culture that promotes thorough post-failure analyses and open discussions about what went wrong without assigning blame will be more effective at learning from setbacks. On the other hand, a culture that rushes to penalize those involved in failures misses the opportunity to extract valuable insights, potentially dooming the organization to repeat its mistakes.

The role of failure in organizational culture is multifaceted, impacting everything from day-to-day operations to long-term strategic planning. Cultures that manage failure effectively can harness it as a powerful driver for learning, innovation, and continuous improvement. Conversely, cultures that fear or stigmatize failure may find themselves stagnating, unable to adapt to new challenges or seize emerging opportunities.

Building a culture that embraces failure as an opportunity requires strategic shifts in organizational mindset, processes, and leadership approaches. Creating such an environment is pivotal for fostering innovation, resilience, and continuous learning. Here are key strategies to cultivate a culture that positively engages with failure:

1. Leadership Role Modeling: It starts at the top. Leaders should openly share their own experiences with failure, emphasizing the lessons learned. By doing so, they set a tone of transparency and vulnerability, making it safe for others to admit and learn from mistakes.

2. Reframing Failure as Learning: Redefine failure not as a setback but as a vital part of the learning process. Encourage teams to view challenges as opportunities to grow. This can be integrated into team meetings, project debriefs, and performance reviews.

3. Encouraging Calculated Risk-Taking: Foster an environment where calculated risks are encouraged. Remove the stigma

associated with failure by celebrating the courage to try new things, even if the outcomes are not always successful.

4. Creating Safe Spaces for Open Dialogue: Develop forums or platforms where employees can openly discuss failures without fear of judgment or retribution. This could be in the form of regular team meetings, workshops, or informal gatherings.

5. Implementing Reflective Practices: Encourage teams to engage in reflective practices such as post-mortem analyses or retrospectives. Focus these sessions on what can be learned and improved, rather than assigning blame.

6. Fostering Support and Collaboration: Build a supportive environment that encourages collaboration. When teams work together and support each other, the fear of failure diminishes, and the collective focus shifts towards finding solutions.

7. Developing Flexible Policies and Processes: Adapt organizational policies and processes to support experimentation and flexibility. This might involve revising project management methodologies or resource allocation to accommodate trial and error.

8. Training and Development: Invest in training programs that focus on skills like resilience, adaptability, and creative problem-solving. These skills are essential for navigating and learning from failures.

9. Celebrating Efforts and Innovations: Recognize and reward efforts and innovations, not just successful outcomes. This recognition can be through formal awards, acknowledgments in meetings, or even informal praise.

10. Continuous Feedback and Improvement: Establish a culture of continuous feedback and improvement. Encourage regular check-ins and feedback sessions that help identify potential issues early and adjust course as needed.

By implementing these strategies, organizations can shift their culture to one that embraces failure as an opportunity for growth and learning. This cultural shift not only enhances innovation and adaptability but also contributes to a more engaged and resilient workforce.

Leadership plays a crucial role in influencing and reshaping organizational culture. The attitudes, behaviors, and values of leaders set a precedent that permeates throughout an organization, shaping its culture significantly. Leaders who understand and embrace this influence can effectively steer their organizations towards desired cultural shifts, including fostering an environment that sees failure as a learning opportunity rather than a setback.

One key way leaders can influence cultural change is through their own behavior. When leaders demonstrate a willingness to take risks, openly discuss their failures, and show vulnerability, they send a powerful message to their teams. This openness can help in creating a safe space where employees feel comfortable sharing ideas and taking risks, knowing that failures are viewed as part of the learning process rather than as causes for punishment or shame.

Leaders can also reshape culture by setting clear expectations and defining new norms. This involves communicating the value of learning from mistakes and encouraging a mindset of continuous improvement. By articulating a vision where calculated risks and innovative thinking are valued, leaders can inspire their teams to adopt these practices. They can influence culture through the policies and procedures they implement. By designing systems that support experimentation and flexibility, leaders can create an environment conducive to learning from failures. This might involve revising project management methodologies, rethinking performance metrics, or adjusting resource allocation strategies to support trial and error.

Training and development initiatives led by leadership are also instrumental in cultural change. By investing in programs that enhance skills like resilience, adaptability, and creative problem-solving, leaders can equip their teams with the tools needed to navigate challenges effectively. This training can help embed these values into the organization's culture.

Leaders can foster cultural change by recognizing and celebrating efforts and innovations, not just successful outcomes. This recognition, whether through formal awards or informal acknowledgments, can reinforce the value placed on learning and innovation. They can drive cultural change by establishing a culture of continuous feedback and improvement. Encouraging regular check-ins and feedback sessions not only helps in identifying potential issues early but also promotes a culture of open communication and continuous development.

Leadership has a profound impact on organizational culture. Through their actions, communications, policies, and the example they set, leaders can cultivate an environment where the fear of failure is minimized, and learning from mistakes is a fundamental part of the organizational ethos.

Fostering a learning environment within an organization is a multifaceted endeavor that involves cultivating a culture where continuous growth and development are prioritized. This requires a strategic approach that integrates various techniques to encourage and support learning at all levels.

Creating a learning environment begins with fostering a mindset of curiosity and openness. Encouraging employees to be curious about their work and the world around them can lead to a more engaged and inquisitive workforce. This can be achieved through regular knowledge-sharing sessions, encouraging employees to attend industry conferences or webinars, or simply promoting open discussions about new ideas and innovations.

Leadership commitment to learning is also vital. When leaders actively engage in their own professional development and share their learning experiences with their teams, it sets a powerful example. Leaders can demonstrate their commitment by participating in training programs alongside their employees or by regularly discussing books, articles, or research relevant to their industry.

Developing a culture of feedback is another important technique. Constructive feedback helps individuals understand their strengths and areas for improvement. Implementing regular performance reviews, 360-degree feedback systems, or peer review mechanisms can facilitate a culture where feedback is openly given and received.

Creating opportunities for experiential learning is also crucial. Employees often learn best by doing, so providing opportunities for hands-on experiences, cross-functional projects, or job rotations can be incredibly beneficial. These experiences allow employees to apply what they have learned in real-world settings, leading to deeper understanding and retention.

Mentorship and coaching programs can also enhance the learning environment. Pairing less experienced employees with more seasoned colleagues or external mentors can provide them with valuable insights, guidance, and support. This one-on-one interaction is not only beneficial for the mentee but also provides an opportunity for mentors to refine their leadership and communication skills.

Investing in learning resources is also key. This might include subscribing to industry journals, building a company library, providing access to online courses, or allocating a budget for professional development. Making these resources readily available and encouraging their use reinforces the importance placed on continuous learning.

Promoting a culture of reflection is essential as well. Encouraging employees to reflect on their experiences, what they've learned, and how they can apply this knowledge in the future is crucial for turning experiences into lasting learning.

Fostering a learning environment requires a comprehensive approach that includes fostering a culture of curiosity, leadership commitment to learning, a culture of feedback, opportunities for experiential learning, mentorship and coaching, investment in learning resources, and promoting a culture of reflection. By integrating these techniques, organizations can create an atmosphere where learning and growth are integral to their culture, leading to continuous improvement and innovation.

In the business world, several companies stand out for their successful cultivation of failure-friendly cultures. These organizations have embraced failure as an integral part of innovation and growth, setting a powerful example for how to foster resilience and adaptability.

- Google: Known for its pioneering approach to innovation, Google has long embraced the philosophy of "failing fast" to succeed sooner. One of its most notable initiatives was the '20% time' policy, which allowed employees to spend a portion of their work time on personal projects. This policy led to the creation of successful products like Gmail and AdSense. Google's approach to failure is characterized by rapid prototyping and iteration, learning quickly from what doesn't work to refine and improve their offerings.

- Pixar Animation Studios: Pixar's culture is built around the belief that failure is a necessary part of creativity and innovation. Ed Catmull, co-founder of Pixar, emphasized the importance of creating a safe environment for people to take risks and fail without fear. The company holds "postmortem" meetings after every movie project, where team members discuss what went wrong and what lessons can be learned, ensuring continuous improvement.

- Amazon: Jeff Bezos, the founder of Amazon, has consistently highlighted the importance of failure in achieving big successes. He attributes much of Amazon's growth to its bold bets and experiments, many of which failed but some of which generated massive success. Amazon Web Services (AWS), now a significant part of Amazon's business, was initially a risky venture that turned out to be highly successful.

- Dyson: The story of Dyson's development of the bagless vacuum cleaner involves over 5,000 failed prototypes. Founder James Dyson's relentless pursuit and willingness to fail were crucial in developing a revolutionary product. This journey exemplifies the company's culture of seeing each failure as a step closer to success.

- 3M: The creation of the Post-it Note at 3M is a classic example of a failure turning into a massive success. The product originated from a failed attempt to create a super-strong adhesive. Instead of writing off this failure, scientists at 3M recognized its potential, leading to the development of one of the most popular office products worldwide. 3M's culture encourages employees to spend 15% of their time exploring their own ideas, reinforcing a culture of creativity and experimentation.

These case studies demonstrate that a positive culture around failure can be a significant driver of innovation and success. By embracing risk-taking, learning from mistakes, and encouraging open dialogue about failures, these companies have fostered environments where employees feel safe to experiment and innovate, leading to breakthrough products and services.

Overcoming cultural barriers to learning from failure within an organization involves recognizing and addressing several common obstacles. One of the primary challenges is the stigma attached to failure, often rooted in traditional notions of success and performance. This stigma can lead to a culture of fear where employees are reluctant to take risks or admit mistakes.

To counter this, organizations need to shift their focus from solely celebrating successes to also recognizing the value of lessons learned from failures. This involves changing the narrative around failure, emphasizing it as a natural and valuable part of the innovation and learning process.

Another obstacle is the lack of open communication and trust. In environments where there is a fear of blame or judgment, employees are less likely to discuss their failures openly. Cultivating an atmosphere of trust and psychological safety, where team members feel secure to share their experiences and learn from each other, is crucial.

Leadership plays a key role in this transformation. Leaders need to model the desired behavior by openly discussing their own failures and the lessons learned. They also need to ensure that systems and processes support this cultural shift, such as implementing fair and constructive feedback mechanisms, and encouraging collaborative problem-solving.

Ongoing education and training can help reinforce the value of learning from failure. Workshops, seminars, and team-building activities focused on resilience, adaptability, and creative thinking can provide employees with the tools and mindset needed to navigate and learn from failures effectively.

Implementing cultural change in an organization is a process that requires deliberate and consistent effort. The first step is to clearly define the desired culture and the values it embodies. This involves engaging in open dialogues with employees at all levels to understand their perspectives and to ensure that the new culture aligns with the organization's goals and values.

Leadership commitment is crucial. Leaders must not only endorse the new culture but also actively demonstrate it through their actions and decisions. This includes recognizing and rewarding behaviors that align with the new culture and addressing those that don't.

Communication is key throughout the process. Regularly communicating the progress, challenges, and successes of the cultural shift helps maintain momentum and buy-in from employees.

Training and development programs that reinforce the new cultural values can be very effective. These programs should focus on skills and behaviors that align with the new culture, such as teamwork, communication, and adaptability.

Finally, regularly reviewing and assessing the cultural change efforts helps ensure that the organization is on the right track. This can involve surveys, feedback sessions, and other tools to gauge employee engagement and to make adjustments as needed.

Successfully implementing cultural change requires a strategic, inclusive, and sustained approach, with a focus on consistent actions, open communication, and ongoing reinforcement.

Measuring the impact of cultural change within an organization involves utilizing various tools and metrics to assess how deeply the change has permeated and its effects on performance and employee engagement. Employee surveys are a common tool, designed to gauge staff perceptions and attitudes towards the new culture. These surveys can cover aspects like job satisfaction, understanding of company values, and comfort in reporting mistakes or failures.

Another metric is the analysis of performance data. Changes in productivity, innovation rates, and the success of new initiatives can indicate how the new culture is influencing work outcomes. Additionally, turnover rates and employee engagement scores provide insight into the culture's impact on staff retention and morale.

360-degree feedback mechanisms also offer valuable insights. By gathering feedback from various levels within the organization, companies can understand how cultural changes are viewed across different departments and hierarchies.

A combination of qualitative and quantitative methods, including surveys, performance data analysis, and feedback systems, is effective in measuring the impact of cultural changes in organizations.

Sustaining a culture of learning and growth in an organization is a dynamic and continuous process. It necessitates not only the initial establishment of cultural values but also their ongoing reinforcement and evolution. This means that leadership must consistently demonstrate and communicate the importance of these values. Sharing success stories and examples of how embracing learning and growth has positively impacted the organization can be a powerful tool in reinforcing these values.

Investing in continuous training and development is key to keeping the culture vibrant. This could involve a range of activities from formal training programs to informal learning sessions and cross-departmental knowledge sharing. Integrating the culture into organizational processes ensures it becomes part of the fabric of the company. This can be achieved by reflecting these values in performance reviews, hiring practices, and reward systems.

A culture of learning and growth thrives on feedback and adaptability. Regularly soliciting and acting on feedback from employees at all levels helps to ensure that the culture remains relevant and effective. It also allows for the identification of areas that may need adjustment or further support.

Sustaining a culture of learning and growth requires a consistent and holistic approach, where the values are not only stated but are lived out in the daily operations and interactions within the organization. It's about creating an environment where continuous improvement is the norm and where every member of the organization feels empowered and equipped to contribute to this ongoing process.

In concluding this chapter, we've delved into the critical role organizational culture plays in framing failure and fostering a learning and growth environment. We've explored how leadership can influence and reshape culture, the importance of creating an environment that embraces failure, and practical steps for initiating and sustaining cultural shifts. The chapter also covered tools and metrics for assessing cultural evolution and strategies for maintaining a culture of learning and growth.

The implications for future organizational strategies are clear: cultivating a positive culture around learning and failure is key to fostering innovation, resilience, and adaptability. Organizations that successfully implement and sustain these cultural changes are likely to be more agile, better equipped to handle challenges, and poised for long-term success. As we move forward, the lessons from this chapter can guide leaders and organizations in nurturing environments where continuous learning and growth are integral to their ethos.

Chapter 4: Analyzing Failures Effectively

In Chapter 4, "Analyzing Failures Effectively," we delve into the processes and strategies essential for understanding and learning from business failures. This chapter emphasizes the importance of thorough failure analysis, which is crucial for any organization striving to improve and innovate. We explore various methodologies for dissecting failures, understanding their root causes, and deriving actionable insights.

This chapter also addresses how to create a culture that does not fear analysis of failures but instead sees it as an opportunity for critical learning and strategic development. The goal is to equip businesses with the tools and mindsets necessary to turn setbacks into springboards for future success. By mastering effective failure analysis, organizations can enhance their resilience, adaptability, and long-term viability in a dynamic business landscape.

Understanding the nature of failure in business is crucial for effective analysis and learning. Business failures can be broadly categorized into several types, each with distinct characteristics and implications.

- Strategic Failures occur when the overarching direction of a business is misguided or poorly executed. This might involve entering an unsuitable market, misjudging customer needs, or failing to adapt to industry changes.

- Operational Failures refer to shortcomings in the day-to-day operations of a business. These can include inefficiencies in processes, quality control issues, or problems with supply chain management.

- Financial Failures are often the most visible and can have immediate impacts. These include cash flow issues, unsustainable debt levels, or poor financial management.

- Innovation Failures arise when new products, services, or processes do not succeed in the market. These failures can be due to misreading market trends, underestimating development challenges, or poor execution of a good idea.

- Leadership and Management Failures stem from poor decision-making, lack of vision, or ineffective management practices. These failures can lead to a demotivated workforce, a lack of clear direction, and ultimately, poor business performance.

- Market Failures occur when external factors such as economic downturns, regulatory changes, or shifts in consumer behavior negatively impact a business.

- Cultural Failures happen when there is a misalignment between the company's values and behaviors, leading to issues like low employee morale, ethical breaches, or a toxic work environment.

Each type of failure requires a unique approach to analysis and remedy. Understanding these distinctions is key to diagnosing issues correctly and applying the right strategies for improvement and avoidance of similar setbacks in the future.

In business, various analytical tools are utilized to conduct effective failure analysis. These tools assist in identifying the root causes of failure and devising strategies to address them.

- A SWOT Analysis serves as a powerful tool for dissecting the multifaceted nature of failure within an organization by evaluating its Strengths, Weaknesses, Opportunities, and Threats. This analytical framework delves deep into understanding the internal and external factors that contribute to setbacks, providing a balanced view of where an organization stands. By identifying internal weaknesses, it pinpoints areas where improvements are necessary and highlights strengths that can be leveraged for recovery and growth. Simultaneously, it scans the external environment for threats that need to be mitigated and opportunities that could be exploited to overcome challenges. This process encourages a strategic approach to decision-making, ensuring that corrective actions are well-informed and targeted towards fostering resilience and sustainable success. Through SWOT Analysis, organizations can develop a comprehensive understanding of their operational landscape, enabling them to formulate strategies that not only address current failures but also position them favorably for future challenges and growth opportunities.

- Root Cause Analysis (RCA) is an in-depth, systematic approach designed to dissect and understand the primary reasons behind failures or problems within an organization. Employing methodologies such as the "5 Whys," this technique involves a thorough interrogation process, where a single question—"Why?"—is asked repeatedly to peel away the layers of symptoms until the foundational cause is unveiled. This method ensures that the investigation goes beyond treating superficial symptoms, focusing instead on identifying and addressing the core issues. By delving into the underlying problems, RCA facilitates the development of effective, sustainable solutions that prevent recurrence of the failure. This comprehensive analysis is crucial for organizations aiming to not only remedy current issues but also fortify their operations against future vulnerabilities. Through the diligent application of RCA, businesses and teams can foster a culture of continuous improvement, enhancing resilience and efficiency by systematically eliminating root causes of failure.

- Failure Mode and Effects Analysis (FMEA) is a structured, proactive approach designed to identify and evaluate potential failures in processes or product designs before they occur. This analytical tool helps in pinpointing possible points of failure, understanding their causes, and assessing the impact of these failures. By systematically analyzing potential failure modes, businesses can prioritize risks based on their severity, likelihood, and detectability, and then devise targeted strategies to mitigate these risks effectively. FMEA facilitates the proactive identification of design or process weaknesses, enabling organizations to implement preventative measures, improve quality, and enhance reliability, thereby ensuring product safety and customer satisfaction. This approach underscores the importance of foresight in risk management, allowing businesses to maintain operational efficiency and competitiveness by minimizing the potential for failure.

- Post-Mortem Analysis is a critical evaluation process conducted after a project or product has not met its objectives, focusing on understanding the sequence of events that led to the failure, identifying the underlying causes, and learning how future projects can avoid similar pitfalls. It involves a detailed examination of the project lifecycle, decisions made, and the outcomes, encouraging an open and honest dialogue among team members. The goal is to foster a culture of transparency and continuous improvement by capturing key insights and integrating them into future initiatives. This analysis not only highlights specific areas for improvement but also reinforces best practices, contributing to organizational learning and resilience. Through meticulous documentation and reflection, Post-Mortem Analysis helps organizations to codify knowledge, ensuring that valuable lessons are applied to enhance the success of subsequent projects.

- The Fishbone Diagram, also known as the Ishikawa diagram, is a visual tool designed to systematically identify and present the potential causes of a specific problem, facilitating the identification of its root causes. It is especially effective in analyzing complex issues that arise from multiple factors. By organizing potential causes into categories such as methods, materials, personnel, and equipment, it allows teams to delve into each aspect of a problem, encouraging thorough analysis and discussion. This method not only helps in pinpointing the underlying causes of problems but also fosters a collaborative approach to problem-solving, making it a valuable tool in quality control and process improvement initiatives. The diagram's structure, resembling the skeleton of a fish, visually maps out the relationships between the problem and its causes, offering clear insights into how different elements interconnect and impact the issue at hand. Through its application, organizations can enhance their diagnostic processes, improve understanding among team members, and develop more effective solutions to complex challenges.

- Pareto Analysis, also known as the 80/20 Rule, is a powerful statistical technique used for decision-making. This principle suggests that 80% of problems are often due to 20% of causes. By applying Pareto Analysis, companies and organizations can identify the most significant factors contributing to a failure or issue. This allows for a focused approach in troubleshooting, enabling teams to prioritize their efforts on the critical issues that have the most substantial impact on performance or outcomes. By concentrating resources on addressing these key areas, organizations can achieve more effective and efficient problem-solving and process improvement. This targeted strategy not only enhances operational efficiency but also significantly improves customer satisfaction and business results. Through the judicious application of Pareto Analysis, businesses can streamline their operations, focusing on making impactful changes that drive substantial improvements across their operations.

Each of these tools offers a unique perspective in analyzing failures, providing valuable insights that can guide strategic improvements and preventive measures.

Effective failure analysis in business is a detailed, multi-step process, essential for learning and improvement. The first step is a thorough information gathering phase. When a failure occurs, it's crucial to collect all relevant data about the event. This includes the specifics of what happened, the timing of the event, and the extent of its impact. Documenting every aspect of the failure provides a solid foundation for deeper analysis.

The next step involves identifying the root causes of the failure. One effective method is Root Cause Analysis (RCA), which requires asking 'why' multiple times until the underlying reason is identified. This technique digs deeper than the surface-level symptoms of the failure, peeling back layers to uncover systemic issues or fundamental errors. This stage demands honesty and often a degree of creativity in thinking, as the true root cause may not be immediately apparent.

Once the root causes are identified, the next phase is the analysis of the collected data. This involves looking for patterns or recurring issues that might indicate larger, systemic problems within the organization. It's important in this stage to remain objective and avoid jumping to conclusions. The analysis should be thorough and unbiased, considering all possible factors that might have contributed to the failure.

Developing a corrective plan is the fourth step. This plan should address both the immediate issues that led to the failure and the underlying systemic problems identified in the analysis phase. The corrective actions should be specific, measurable, and achievable. It's important to set clear timelines and responsibilities for implementing these actions to ensure accountability.

The final step is implementing the changes and monitoring their effectiveness. This phase involves putting the corrective plan into action and closely observing the outcomes to ensure that the changes are effective. Continuous monitoring is key, as it allows for adjustments to be made if the initial plan doesn't yield the expected results. This step closes the loop in the failure analysis process, ensuring that the organization not only learns from its failures but also systematically improves its practices and processes to prevent future occurrences.

There are several notable real-world examples of successful failure analysis that have led to significant improvements and innovations.

The Apollo 13 mission, regarded as a "successful failure" by NASA, turned a near-disastrous event into a case study of resilience, innovation, and teamwork. Following the explosion of an oxygen tank, NASA's mission control and the Apollo 13 crew had to work together ingeniously to solve complex problems in real-time, ensuring the safe return of the astronauts. This incident prompted a thorough analysis that led to significant advancements in spacecraft design, safety protocols, and mission planning. These improvements were crucial for enhancing the robustness and reliability of subsequent missions, demonstrating the critical role of learning from failures in advancing human space exploration.

The subsequent failure analysis uncovered technical flaws and procedural gaps that contributed to the crisis, leading to comprehensive revisions in spacecraft engineering and astronaut training programs. By addressing these issues, NASA could mitigate similar risks in future missions, contributing to the overall safety and success of its space exploration endeavors. This proactive approach to failure management underscored the importance of a culture that prioritizes continuous improvement and risk assessment in complex, high-stakes environments.

The Apollo 13 mission exemplifies the importance of adaptability and problem-solving under pressure. The successful resolution of the crisis, achieved through the collaborative efforts of the crew and an extensive support team on the ground, highlighted the human capacity to overcome seemingly insurmountable challenges through creativity and perseverance. This mission remains a testament to the enduring spirit of exploration and innovation that drives space exploration, offering valuable lessons for managing crises and advancing technology in pursuit of human achievements beyond our planet.

Toyota's response to its quality control issues, which led to widespread recalls, serves as a notable example of proactive crisis management and improvement in corporate practices. The automotive giant undertook a comprehensive failure analysis that pinpointed the deficiencies in its quality control processes. This rigorous examination was the catalyst for a series of reforms aimed at enhancing the robustness of Toyota's quality assurance mechanisms, ensuring such issues would be significantly reduced or prevented in the future.

Recognizing the critical importance of customer trust, Toyota renewed its commitment to safety and satisfaction, implementing stringent quality control measures and enhancing its oversight of production processes. These steps were part of a broader strategy to rebuild the company's reputation and ensure the highest standards of product reliability. Toyota's initiative to transparently address and rectify the causes of the recalls demonstrated its dedication to upholding and prioritizing the welfare of its customers.

Toyota's actions reflected a larger corporate philosophy shift towards continuous improvement and responsiveness to consumer feedback. By integrating lessons learned from the recalls into its operational ethos, Toyota reinforced its position as a leader in automotive innovation and customer service. This approach not only helped to restore confidence among consumers and stakeholders but also set new benchmarks for quality and reliability in the automotive industry.

In addition to internal reforms, Toyota's engagement with regulatory bodies and commitment to transparency played a vital role in the recovery process. The company worked closely with safety organizations and regulators to ensure that its corrective measures met and exceeded industry standards, demonstrating its responsibility and commitment to public safety.

Toyota's handling of the recall crisis underscores the significance of adaptive crisis management and the value of a customer-centric approach in overcoming challenges. By focusing on comprehensive analysis, quality improvement, and transparent communication, Toyota successfully navigated the repercussions of the recalls, emerging as a more resilient and trusted brand committed to excellence in quality and safety.

In the pharmaceutical industry, the development of new drugs is a process fraught with challenges and frequent failures. Each failed drug trial, while a setback, generates a wealth of data that is invaluable to researchers. This data is meticulously analyzed to understand what went wrong and why, providing critical insights that inform future research efforts.

The insights gained from these analyses are used to refine research hypotheses, leading to adjustments in study designs, dosing regimens, and target populations for subsequent trials. This iterative process of learning from failure is fundamental to the scientific method and is particularly crucial in the high-stakes world of drug development.

Over time, the accumulation of knowledge from failed trials contributes to a deeper understanding of diseases and their interactions with potential treatments. This enhanced understanding is essential for designing more effective and targeted future trials, increasing the likelihood of success.

Eventually, through this rigorous process of hypothesis testing, analysis, and refinement, breakthroughs are achieved, leading to the development of successful treatments. These successes often come after many rounds of failure and iteration, but each failure is a stepping stone towards the ultimate goal of finding effective therapies.

This approach underscores the importance of resilience and persistence in the pharmaceutical industry. It highlights how failures, while initially disappointing, are invaluable learning opportunities that pave the way for future successes.

Thus, the pharmaceutical industry's reliance on learning from failed drug trials exemplifies a broader principle applicable in many fields: that failure is not just an obstacle to be avoided but a vital source of information that can drive progress and innovation.

The cases of NASA's Apollo 13 mission, Toyota's quality control issues, and the pharmaceutical industry's drug development process each exemplify the importance of analyzing failures effectively to drive improvement and innovation. NASA's Apollo 13 mission demonstrates how a critical failure led to significant advancements in spacecraft design and operational procedures, ensuring the safety and success of future space missions. This case highlights the value of thorough investigation and adaptive problem-solving in high-stakes environments.

Toyota's response to its recall crisis showcases the significance of identifying and addressing the root causes of failures. By implementing comprehensive changes to its quality control processes, Toyota not only resolved the immediate issues but also reinforced its commitment to customer safety and satisfaction. This example underlines the importance of organizational commitment to continuous improvement and customer-centric values in maintaining brand integrity.

The pharmaceutical industry's approach to drug development illustrates how failures can be leveraged as opportunities for learning and refinement. Each failed drug trial provides valuable data that, when analyzed, contributes to refining research hypotheses and improving future trials. This process emphasizes the iterative nature of scientific research and the critical role of persistence and resilience in achieving breakthroughs.

Analyzing failures effectively requires a culture that views setbacks not as insurmountable obstacles but as sources of invaluable insights. This perspective enables organizations to turn challenges into catalysts for growth and innovation. Whether in space exploration, automotive manufacturing, or pharmaceutical research, the ability to learn from failure and adapt strategies accordingly is a key driver of success.

These cases illustrate the necessity of a supportive infrastructure that encourages open discussion of failures and a systematic approach to analyzing them. Organizations that foster an environment where failures are openly examined and lessons are integrated into future plans are better positioned to innovate and remain competitive.

The analysis of failures across different industries reveals a common theme: the path to success is often paved with setbacks. By embracing failures as opportunities to learn and improve, organizations can turn challenges into stepping stones towards excellence and innovation.

Developing analytical skills in executives is not only about enhancing their ability to interpret data but also about fostering a mindset attuned to critical thinking and problem-solving. Encouraging executives to continuously seek new knowledge and perspectives is crucial. This can be achieved through regular exposure to diverse business scenarios, cross-industry learning, and keeping abreast of global market trends. Such exposure broadens their understanding and equips them with a more nuanced approach to analysis.

Structured training programs are another cornerstone in developing analytical skills. These programs should focus on critical thinking, data interpretation, and strategic planning. Incorporating modules on emerging technologies, market analytics, and business intelligence tools can provide executives with the technical skills required for in-depth analysis. Case studies, workshops, and interactive sessions led by industry experts can make these training programs more engaging and practical.

Mentorship and coaching play a significant role in honing an executive's analytical capabilities. Experienced leaders, with their wealth of knowledge and insights, can guide executives through complex problem-solving processes. They can provide personalized feedback, share experiences of navigating business challenges, and offer strategies for effective decision-making.

This one-on-one interaction not only enhances analytical skills but also helps in developing leadership qualities.

Real-world application and reflective practices are key to solidifying these skills. Engaging executives in real-world problem-solving scenarios, such as business simulations or strategy development exercises, allows them to apply their learning in a controlled, risk-free environment. Regular feedback sessions and self-reflection exercises help executives understand their analytical strengths and weaknesses, fostering a culture of continuous improvement and learning. This comprehensive approach, blending education, real-world application, mentorship, and reflective practices, ensures that executives develop robust analytical skills that are crucial for successful leadership in today's dynamic business landscape.

In concluding Chapter 4, "Analyzing Failures Effectively," we've gained comprehensive insights into the critical role of failure analysis in business. We've explored the various types of business failures, each with unique characteristics and impacts, and how understanding these nuances is key to effective analysis. The chapter introduced a range of analytical tools and methodologies designed to dissect and learn from these setbacks.

We discussed the importance of cultivating strong analytical skills among executives. The strategies outlined for enhancing these skills, from continuous learning to practical problem-solving exercises, emphasize the necessity of a well-rounded approach to decision-making and strategic planning.

The implications of this chapter for business success are profound. Organizations that master the art of analyzing failures are poised not only to avoid similar pitfalls in the future but also to leverage these experiences for greater innovation and strategic foresight. This capability is especially crucial in today's rapidly changing business environment, where adaptability and learning from past experiences can provide a significant competitive edge.

This chapter highlights that the path to enduring success in business is often paved with the lessons learned from past failures. By embracing a culture that prioritizes effective failure analysis and continuous skill development in analytical thinking, businesses can transform potential setbacks into catalysts for growth, resilience, and long-term success.

Chapter 5: Strategic Responses to Failure

In the dynamic world of business, encountering failure is not a matter of if, but when. Every leader, regardless of their experience or industry, will inevitably face moments of strategic setback. However, what sets successful leaders apart is their ability to respond strategically to these failures. This chapter delves into the critical topic of "Strategic Responses to Failure" and aims to equip leaders with the knowledge and tools necessary to transform setbacks into opportunities for growth and resilience.

Before we explore the various strategic responses to failure, it is crucial to understand what constitutes strategic failure in the first place. We will analyze the different dimensions of strategic failure, from poor decision-making to external factors beyond our control. By gaining a clear understanding of the root causes, leaders can better assess and address their specific situations.

In the wake of a failure, leaders often find themselves at a crossroads – do they stick to their original planned strategies or pivot towards more adaptive approaches? This section will guide leaders on navigating this delicate balance. It's essential to recognize the value of deliberate planning while remaining open to emergent strategies that may arise organically from the experience of failure.

Effective management and reallocation of resources are critical after experiencing a setback. Leaders need to make informed decisions about where to invest, cut back, or redirect resources. We will explore strategies for optimizing resource allocation in the aftermath of failure, ensuring that valuable assets are directed toward the most promising opportunities.

One of the key lessons from failure is the importance of being prepared for various business outcomes. This section will introduce techniques for scenario planning, enabling leaders to anticipate and strategize for different potential scenarios. By thinking ahead and developing strategies for multiple possibilities, leaders can enhance their adaptability and resilience.

In the world of business, uncertainties and risks are constant companions. Leaders must be proactive in creating contingency plans to mitigate future risks and failures. We will discuss the process of developing robust contingency strategies that can be activated swiftly when needed, ensuring that the organization remains agile and responsive to challenges.

This chapter will provide a summary of the key strategic responses to failure discussed throughout the text. It will underline the importance of these responses in bolstering business resilience and ensuring that leaders are better equipped to transform setbacks into steppingstones toward future success. By embracing strategic responses to failure, leaders can harness the power of adversity and emerge stronger, more adaptive, and more resilient than ever before.

Strategic responses to failure in business are essential for turning setbacks into opportunities for growth and resilience. This section will review key strategies and responses to them in detail.

Understanding strategic failure requires leaders to conduct a comprehensive analysis of the circumstances leading to underperformance or setbacks within their organizations. This process begins with identifying the specific nature of the failure, whether it stems from internal decision-making errors, flawed strategies, or external pressures such as market dynamics or competitive actions. It's crucial to delve into the underlying causes of these issues, distinguishing between factors that are controllable and those that are not.

Once the root causes are identified, leaders must evaluate the impact of these failures on the organization's objectives and operations. This involves assessing the short-term and long-term repercussions on financial performance, market position, and organizational reputation. Understanding the breadth and depth of strategic failure enables leaders to gauge the urgency and scope of the response needed.

Developing a response to strategic failure involves formulating a plan that addresses the identified causes and mitigates their effects. This may include revising existing strategies, implementing new processes, or even redefining organizational goals to align with the current reality. Leaders must be willing to make tough decisions, such as reallocating resources or pivoting from previously set paths, to steer their organizations back toward success.

Communication plays a pivotal role in managing strategic failure. Leaders must effectively communicate the nature of the failure, its implications, and the steps being taken to address it to all stakeholders, including employees, investors, and customers. Transparent and honest communication helps to rebuild trust and ensures that everyone within the organization is aligned with the recovery efforts.

Learning from strategic failure is essential for organizational growth and resilience. This requires not just a post-mortem analysis of what went wrong but also a commitment to incorporating these lessons into future strategic planning and decision-making processes. By understanding and addressing the factors that led to strategic failure, leaders can better position their organizations to navigate challenges and capitalize on opportunities in the future.

After experiencing failure, leaders are faced with a critical decision: adhere to their meticulously laid plans or shift towards more flexible, emergent strategies. This juncture demands a strategic balance, recognizing when to persist with the original course and when to adapt to new insights and circumstances. Successful navigation post-failure often requires integrating deliberate planning with the agility to seize unforeseen opportunities, allowing organizations to remain resilient and responsive to dynamic market conditions.

Deliberate strategies entail a clear, planned approach designed to achieve specific goals. However, sticking rigidly to these plans in the face of failure can sometimes hinder recovery and growth. On the other hand, emergent strategies arise spontaneously from within the organization, adapting to current realities without a predetermined plan. These strategies can offer innovative solutions and directions that were not initially considered.

The challenge for leaders is to create an environment where both approaches coexist harmoniously. By fostering a culture that values both planning and flexibility, leaders can encourage a proactive stance towards unexpected opportunities while maintaining a clear vision and purpose. This balance enables organizations to leverage their strengths effectively while remaining agile enough to navigate and learn from failures.

Incorporating feedback mechanisms to continuously assess the effectiveness of strategies in real-time is crucial. These mechanisms help identify when a deliberate strategy is failing to meet its objectives and when emergent strategies are beginning to show promise. This ongoing evaluation ensures that the organization can pivot quickly, aligning its actions with the most effective approach to achieve its goals.

Balancing these strategies requires open communication and a willingness to experiment and take calculated risks. Leaders must champion a mindset of innovation and resilience, encouraging teams to explore new ideas and approaches without fear of failure. This approach not only aids in recovering from setbacks but also positions the organization for long-term success by cultivating adaptability and a forward-thinking outlook.

The ability to balance deliberate and emergent strategies hinges on leadership's capacity to navigate complexity and uncertainty. By embracing both planned and adaptive approaches, leaders can guide their organizations through challenges, leveraging failures as opportunities for growth and innovation. This balanced strategy ensures that organizations are not only prepared to face immediate issues but are also poised to capitalize on future opportunities.

After a failure, the strategic reallocation of resources becomes a critical task for leadership. Decisions on where to invest, cut back, or redirect resources require a deep understanding of the organization's current state and its future potential. Effective resource allocation ensures that valuable assets are focused on areas with the highest return on investment, enabling the organization to recover and capitalize on new opportunities.

Leaders must evaluate the organization's capabilities and resources in light of the failure, identifying underperforming areas that may no longer align with strategic objectives. This evaluation often leads to tough decisions, such as reducing investments in certain projects or departments, to free up resources for more promising initiatives. It's a process that requires careful consideration of both short-term needs and long-term goals.

At the same time, redirecting resources towards areas with potential for growth or innovation can spark a turnaround. Investing in new technologies, markets, or product development could open up avenues for success that were previously unexplored. Leaders need to be visionary, recognizing emerging opportunities and positioning their organization to take advantage of them.

However, resource reallocation is not just about financial investment. It also involves the strategic deployment of human capital. Leaders should consider how to best utilize the skills and talents of their team, moving personnel to roles where they can make the most significant impact. This might involve training or development programs to enhance capabilities aligned with the new strategic direction.

Ultimately, effective resource allocation after failure is about making informed, strategic decisions that set the organization on a path to recovery and growth. Leaders must be adaptable, willing to make difficult choices, and savvy in identifying and seizing new opportunities. By doing so, they can turn a period of failure into a launching pad for future success.

Scenario planning is a strategic tool that enables leaders to enhance their organization's adaptability and resilience by preparing for various future possibilities. This technique involves envisioning different potential scenarios that the organization might face, ranging from the most likely to the highly speculative. By doing so, leaders can identify potential challenges and opportunities that may arise, allowing them to develop strategic responses in advance.

This process of scenario planning encourages a forward-looking mindset, prompting leaders to consider not just immediate plans but also long-term strategies that account for a range of external variables. Factors such as market trends, economic fluctuations, technological advancements, and regulatory changes are all considered in developing these scenarios. This comprehensive approach ensures that the organization is better equipped to navigate the uncertainties of the future.

Through scenario planning, organizations can create flexible strategies that are robust enough to withstand various future states. This flexibility is crucial for maintaining a competitive edge and achieving sustained success in an ever-changing business environment. By anticipating different futures, leaders can allocate resources more effectively, prioritize initiatives that bolster resilience, and avoid being caught off-guard by unexpected developments.

Moreover, engaging in scenario planning fosters a culture of strategic thinking and continuous learning within the organization. It encourages teams across the organization to contribute their insights and perspectives, enriching the scenario planning process and building a collective understanding of potential futures. This collaborative approach enhances the organization's collective ability to respond to changes proactively rather than reactively.

Ultimately, scenario planning is not about predicting the future with certainty but about preparing the organization to thrive in a variety of future states. It empowers leaders to make informed decisions, adapt strategies quickly, and navigate the complexities of the business landscape with confidence. By incorporating scenario planning into their strategic toolkit, leaders can ensure their organizations are poised for success, regardless of what the future holds.

In today's unpredictable business landscape, the development of contingency strategies is a critical component of organizational resilience. Leaders must proactively design these plans with a clear understanding of potential risks and vulnerabilities their organizations might face. This foresight enables the creation of specific actions and protocols that can be rapidly implemented in response to various crises, ensuring that the organization can maintain operational continuity and mitigate the impacts of unforeseen events.

Contingency strategies are more than just backup plans; they are comprehensive approaches that prepare an organization for multiple scenarios, including financial downturns, supply chain disruptions, technological failures, and other critical risks. By identifying these potential threats in advance, leaders can establish a framework for decision-making that allows for quick, informed responses. This preparedness is invaluable in preserving the integrity and stability of the organization during times of crisis.

The agility and responsiveness afforded by well-developed contingency plans give organizations a competitive advantage. In the face of adversity, the ability to pivot and adapt quickly can mean the difference between surviving and thriving. These strategies ensure that resources are allocated efficiently, communication lines are clear, and employees understand their roles and responsibilities, minimizing chaos and confusion during critical periods.

The process of developing contingency strategies encourages a culture of strategic thinking and risk awareness throughout the organization. It involves collaboration across departments, enhancing the overall strategic alignment and fostering a sense of unity and purpose. This collaborative effort not only enriches the contingency planning process but also strengthens the organization's collective ability to face challenges head-on.

Effective contingency planning also involves regular review and updates to ensure that the strategies remain relevant and effective in the face of changing external conditions and internal capabilities. This continuous improvement cycle ensures that the organization can evolve its response mechanisms in tandem with its growth and the dynamic nature of business risks.

Developing robust contingency strategies is essential for organizations aiming to navigate the complexities of the modern business environment successfully. By preparing for the unexpected, leaders can safeguard their organizations against potential threats, ensuring agility, stability, and resilience in the face of challenges. This proactive approach to risk management is fundamental to securing long-term success and sustainability.

In addressing strategic failures, it's crucial for leaders to recognize and learn from past mistakes, dynamically adapt to evolving market conditions, and cultivate resilience for sustained business success. Strategic failure, in essence, is the shortfall in achieving desired outcomes due to various internal and external factors, including misaligned business strategies, flawed decision-making, and external market pressures. Such failures necessitate a deep dive into the root causes, be they misjudgments, execution gaps, or inadequate responses to feedback and changing scenarios.

Organizations often encounter strategic missteps when their implemented actions diverge from the core objectives and visions, a scenario that can stem from vague goals or an inflexibility to pivot as situations change. The decision-making process is another critical area where failures occur, influenced by reliance on insufficient data, cognitive biases, or neglecting foreseeable risks. Moreover, the external business environment, including market dynamics, regulatory changes, and unforeseen competition, plays a significant role in shaping strategic success or failure.

A key to navigating strategic failure is the organization's agility and its ability to respond to changes promptly. An inherent resistance to change or a lack of adaptive mechanisms can severely hamper an organization's ability to address emerging challenges or capitalize on new opportunities. Thus, fostering a culture that encourages agility, continuous learning, and openness to stakeholder feedback is paramount.

The synthesis of strategic planning tools and methodologies, such as SWOT Analysis, Root Cause Analysis, and Failure Mode and Effects Analysis, with forward-looking practices like Scenario Planning and the development of Contingency Strategies, equips leaders with the insights and flexibility needed to steer their organizations towards resilience and success. These practices encourage a proactive stance on future planning, risk management, and strategic alignment with organizational goals.

Overcoming strategic failures demands an integrated approach that combines learning from past setbacks with a proactive anticipation of future challenges. By instilling a culture of strategic reflection, continuous improvement, and adaptability, leaders can ensure their organizations not only recover from failures but also thrive in an ever-changing business landscape, securing long-term growth and stability.

Even well-conceived strategies can fail if they are not executed effectively. Inadequate implementation, a lack of progress monitoring, and an inability to make necessary adjustments can contribute to strategic failure. Ignoring valuable input from employees, customers, and stakeholders can lead to strategic missteps. Incorporating feedback from those directly involved can help identify blind spots in decision-making. A failure to learn from previous mistakes and apply those lessons to future strategies is a common cause of recurring strategic failures. Establishing a culture of continuous improvement is essential for avoiding repeated setbacks.

Understanding these dimensions of strategic failure is crucial for leaders. It enables them to diagnose the root causes of setbacks and develop targeted responses and strategies to mitigate failure's impact, ultimately paving the way for more successful endeavors. In the aftermath of a business failure, leaders are confronted with the crucial task of striking a delicate balance between deliberate and emergent strategies. To effectively navigate this terrain, it is imperative to begin with a thorough assessment of the factors that contributed to the failure, gaining a comprehensive understanding of the root causes. This assessment provides the foundation for evaluating the initial deliberate strategies and identifying areas that require adjustments or enhancements to align with the current business landscape.

Recognizing the significance of adaptability is paramount in today's ever-evolving business environment. Leaders must be prepared to modify or even discard aspects of the original plan that have become obsolete or ineffective in the present context. Engaging key stakeholders, including employees, partners, and customers, in discussions about strategy adaptation is essential, as their insights can offer valuable input.

Remaining vigilant in monitoring market dynamics, such as trends, competitive developments, and external factors, allows organizations to spot opportunities for emergent strategies to capitalize on new prospects. It is advisable to pilot and test emergent strategies on a smaller scale before full-scale implementation to minimize risks.

Adopting a culture of continuous learning and improvement is indispensable. Leaders should assess the effectiveness of both deliberate and emergent strategies continually, being prepared to iterate and refine them based on ongoing feedback and results. Effective communication plays a pivotal role in this process, ensuring that the entire organization comprehends the rationale behind the shift from deliberate to emergent strategies.

Maintaining a balance between the stability provided by deliberate strategies and the adaptability of emergent strategies is crucial.

Excessive shifts in either direction can introduce instability. Finally, emphasizing agility throughout the organization by encouraging employees to proactively identify opportunities and adapt to changing circumstances is instrumental in responding not only to failures but also to emerging opportunities in the competitive business landscape. In sum, finding the right equilibrium between deliberate and emergent strategies post-failure requires a strategic and well-communicated approach, allowing organizations to respond effectively to setbacks and position themselves for future success.

In the wake of a business setback or failure, leaders are tasked with the critical challenge of managing and reallocating resources effectively. This process plays a pivotal role in not only recovering from the setback but also charting a course for future success. The initial step involves a comprehensive assessment of the organization's existing resources, encompassing financial assets, human capital, and technological infrastructure.

This assessment provides a clear understanding of available resources and helps identify any gaps or deficiencies that may have contributed to the failure. Leaders must then prioritize resource allocation, aligning it with the revised business strategy and critical recovery needs. Cost-benefit analysis becomes essential, weighing potential returns against the costs involved in reallocating resources. Developing systematic reallocation strategies, such as shifting budgets or reassigning personnel, is crucial to ensuring that resources are in sync with the organization's new strategic direction.

Human resources should not be underestimated in this process, as their deployment to roles where expertise can have a significant impact is pivotal. Continuous monitoring and evaluation mechanisms are put in place to track the effectiveness of resource allocation decisions and provide ongoing insights for adjustment. Flexibility is crucial, allowing leaders to adapt resource allocation to emerging opportunities or challenges. Clear and transparent communication with all stakeholders is paramount, ensuring buy-in and alignment with resource allocation changes.

Mitigating potential risks associated with reallocation, such as disruptions to ongoing projects or employee morale, is part of a comprehensive approach. Lastly, leaders should balance addressing immediate recovery needs with long-term sustainability, ensuring that resources are allocated to support the organization's resilience and growth over time. In conclusion, effective resource allocation post-failure requires a systematic and strategic approach, encompassing assessment, prioritization, cost-benefit analysis, reallocation strategies, monitoring, flexibility, communication, risk mitigation, and long-term planning. By managing resources strategically, organizations can enhance their ability to recover from setbacks and position themselves for sustainable growth and success.

Preparing for various business outcomes is a fundamental aspect of strategic planning and risk management. Organizations must be equipped with techniques that allow them to anticipate and respond effectively to a range of scenarios. One essential technique is scenario planning, where multiple plausible future scenarios are developed based on different variables and assumptions. This approach enables organizations to identify potential challenges and opportunities and formulate strategies to address them.

Another valuable technique is stress testing, which involves subjecting the business to hypothetical adverse conditions to assess its resilience. By simulating worst-case scenarios, organizations can identify vulnerabilities and take proactive steps to strengthen their operations. Market research and competitive analysis are critical techniques for understanding external dynamics. By continuously monitoring market trends, customer behavior, and competitive landscape, businesses can adapt their strategies in response to changing conditions.

Organizations can engage in contingency planning, which involves developing predefined responses and action plans for specific adverse events. These plans serve as a playbook for rapid and effective decision-making during crises.

Effective resource management and diversification strategies are essential techniques for preparing for various business outcomes. Ensuring that resources are allocated efficiently and having a diversified portfolio of products, services, and revenue streams can mitigate risks associated with reliance on a single source.

Lastly, fostering a culture of innovation and adaptability is a technique that underpins preparedness for various business outcomes. Organizations that encourage employees to think creatively and embrace change are better equipped to pivot and thrive in uncertain environments.

In conclusion, preparing for various business outcomes requires a multi-faceted approach that encompasses scenario planning, stress testing, market research, competitive analysis, contingency planning, resource management, diversification, and a culture of innovation. These techniques enable organizations to proactively address challenges, seize opportunities, and enhance their resilience in an ever-evolving business landscape.

Developing contingency strategies is a critical aspect of strategic planning in business. These strategies involve creating plans to mitigate future risks and failures, ensuring that organizations are prepared to respond effectively to unexpected events.

Contingency planning begins with identifying potential risks and failures that could impact the organization. These risks can encompass a wide range of scenarios, including economic downturns, supply chain disruptions, natural disasters, regulatory changes, and more. By conducting a thorough risk assessment, businesses can pinpoint areas of vulnerability.

Once risks are identified, organizations develop specific contingency plans tailored to each scenario. These plans outline the steps to be taken in response to a particular risk or failure, including the allocation of resources, communication strategies, and decision-making processes. They also establish clear roles and responsibilities for individuals or teams responsible for executing the plan.

Regular testing and simulation exercises are essential components of contingency planning. By conducting drills and simulations, organizations can assess the effectiveness of their contingency plans and identify any weaknesses that need to be addressed. This iterative process ensures that plans are robust and can be executed seamlessly when needed.

Effective communication is a cornerstone of successful contingency planning. Organizations must ensure that employees, stakeholders, and relevant parties are aware of the contingency plans and understand their roles in implementing them. Clear and timely communication during a crisis is vital for maintaining trust and minimizing disruption.

Contingency strategies also involve financial preparedness. This includes setting aside reserves or establishing lines of credit that can be tapped into during a crisis to ensure the organization's financial stability and ability to execute the contingency plan.

Developing contingency strategies is an essential part of risk management and business resilience. These plans provide a roadmap for mitigating future risks and failures, helping organizations respond effectively to unexpected events. Through risk assessment, plan development, testing, clear communication, and financial preparedness, businesses can enhance their ability to weather crises and continue operating successfully in an unpredictable business environment.

The strategic responses highlighted in this chapter are crucial for bolstering business resilience and achieving sustained success amid a fast-paced and competitive environment. A deep understanding of strategic failure lays the groundwork for effectively overcoming challenges, emphasizing the importance of both recognizing and learning from setbacks. The ability to balance deliberate planning with the flexibility to adopt emergent strategies ensures organizations can remain agile and aligned with their core objectives despite changing circumstances. Post-failure resource allocation is critical for directing efforts and investments towards areas with the highest potential for growth and recovery.

Scenario planning and the development of contingency strategies further equip businesses to anticipate a variety of future scenarios, enhancing preparedness for different potential outcomes. These strategies enable organizations to proactively address risks and adapt to failures, highlighting the significance of foresight and strategic risk management. Collectively, these approaches create a robust framework that enables leaders to navigate through adversity, fostering a culture of adaptability, continuous improvement, and strategic resilience.

In an era characterized by constant change and uncertainty, the capacity for strategic response to failure distinguishes resilient and thriving businesses from the rest. Embracing these strategic responses transforms setbacks into opportunities for development, positioning organizations to successfully navigate the complexities of the business world. Leaders who adopt these practices not only pave the way for immediate recovery but also lay the foundations for long-term prosperity, ensuring their organizations are well-prepared to face future challenges and seize opportunities in the evolving business landscape.

Chapter 6: Innovating Through Failures

In the dynamic landscape of business, innovation is often considered the lifeblood of growth and competitiveness. However, what is often overlooked is the intrinsic connection between innovation and failure. This chapter delves into the significance of innovation through the lens of failure, showcasing how setbacks and missteps can become catalysts for transformative and creative solutions. We will explore the critical role of experimentation in driving innovation, the importance of embracing risk-taking, and how learning from failure can fuel creativity.

Through in-depth case studies, we will profile companies that have harnessed the power of innovation born from failure, highlighting their journey from setbacks to groundbreaking successes. Additionally, we will discuss strategies for fostering an innovative culture within organizations following setbacks, emphasizing the need for adaptability and a forward-thinking mindset.

This chapter also equips readers with practical tools and methodologies for innovating through failures, providing actionable insights that can be applied in real-world business scenarios. Ultimately, it underscores the vital role of failure as a stepping stone toward innovation and future success in an ever-evolving business landscape.

Innovation and failure may seem like contrasting concepts, but in the world of business, they are deeply intertwined. In fact, innovation often finds its most fertile ground in the aftermath of failure. When viewed through this lens, failure takes on a new significance as a powerful catalyst for creative and transformative innovation.

First and foremost, failure serves as a crucial learning experience. When businesses encounter setbacks or failures, they are forced to analyze what went wrong, why it happened, and what could have been done differently. This introspection is a key driver of innovation. It prompts organizations to question the status quo, challenge existing assumptions, and seek alternative solutions.

Failure also encourages risk-taking and experimentation. When businesses recognize that not every initiative will succeed, they become more willing to explore unconventional ideas and approaches. The fear of failure diminishes, allowing for a culture of experimentation to flourish. It's often through these experiments, even the unsuccessful ones, that groundbreaking innovations emerge.

Moreover, failure fosters resilience. Organizations that have weathered failures are often more adaptable and better prepared to navigate future challenges. This adaptability is a critical element of innovation. It allows businesses to pivot, seize new opportunities, and stay ahead of competitors in a rapidly changing market.

Failure can also serve as a source of motivation and inspiration. When faced with adversity, individuals and teams often tap into their creativity and resourcefulness to find solutions. This drive to overcome obstacles can lead to the development of innovative products, services, or processes that might not have been explored in the absence of failure.

Innovation through the lens of failure is not about celebrating setbacks but rather recognizing that they are an integral part of the journey toward progress. It's about embracing failure as a valuable teacher, a springboard for creativity, and a catalyst for growth. Businesses that understand the significance of innovation through the lens of failure are more likely to thrive in today's ever-changing business landscape, where adaptability and creative problem-solving are essential for success.

Experimentation lies at the heart of innovation in the business world. It is a dynamic and iterative process that allows organizations to explore new ideas, test hypotheses, and uncover opportunities for improvement. This approach is not limited to laboratories; it is a powerful tool for driving innovation and fostering growth in various aspects of business.

One of the primary ways in which experimentation leads to innovation is by encouraging a culture of curiosity and exploration. When businesses embrace experimental approaches, they create an environment where employees are encouraged to ask questions, challenge assumptions, and think creatively. This mindset shift is essential for generating innovative ideas and solutions.

Experimentation also promotes a willingness to take calculated risks. By nature, experiments involve a degree of uncertainty, but they are not undertaken blindly. Instead, they are based on careful planning, data collection, and analysis. This calculated risk-taking allows organizations to push boundaries and explore new territories, leading to breakthrough innovations.

Furthermore, experimentation fosters a deeper understanding of customers and markets. By testing different strategies, products, or services, businesses gain valuable insights into what resonates with their target audience. This customer-centric approach not only leads to better product-market fit but also opens doors to new opportunities and markets.

Innovation often arises from unexpected outcomes. Through experimentation, businesses can stumble upon solutions and ideas they might not have considered in a traditional, linear approach to problem-solving. These "happy accidents" can lead to groundbreaking innovations that change the trajectory of a company.

Another critical aspect of experimentation is rapid iteration. By continually testing and refining ideas, businesses can adapt to changing circumstances and market conditions more effectively.

This agility is essential in a fast-paced business environment where staying ahead of competitors is crucial.

The role of experimentation in business is pivotal for driving innovation. It encourages a culture of curiosity, calculated risk-taking, customer-centricity, and adaptability. Through experimentation, organizations can uncover new ideas, refine existing ones, and ultimately create innovative solutions that propel them forward in the ever-evolving business landscape. It's not just a process; it's a mindset that fuels growth and success.

Risk-taking and innovation are intrinsically linked in the world of business. Embracing risk is not merely a choice; it is a fundamental requirement for driving growth and staying competitive in dynamic markets. Understanding the importance of risk-taking is pivotal to unlocking the full potential of innovation.

First and foremost, risk-taking in innovation is about challenging the status quo. It involves questioning established norms, experimenting with untested ideas, and venturing into the unknown. While these endeavors carry inherent uncertainties, they also present the opportunity for groundbreaking discoveries and advancements.

Innovation often thrives in an environment where calculated risks are welcomed. When businesses encourage employees to take risks, they foster a culture of creativity and bold problem-solving. This mindset shift empowers teams to explore unconventional approaches and think outside the box, leading to innovative breakthroughs.

Risk-taking is integral to staying ahead of the competition. In today's rapidly evolving business landscape, companies that rest on their laurels and avoid risks may find themselves left behind. Embracing calculated risks allows organizations to seize opportunities, enter new markets, and differentiate themselves from competitors.

Risk-taking in innovation also encourages resilience. When businesses understand that not every risk will yield immediate success, they become better equipped to weather setbacks and failures. These experiences, while challenging, often serve as valuable learning opportunities that inform future strategies and innovations.

Embracing risk-taking enhances adaptability. In a world where change is constant, the ability to pivot and adjust quickly is a strategic advantage. Organizations that are open to taking risks are more agile and better equipped to respond to shifting market dynamics and emerging trends.

It's crucial to emphasize that risk-taking in innovation should be calculated and informed. It is not about reckless decision-making but rather about making well-informed choices based on data, market insights, and a thorough understanding of potential outcomes.

Understanding the importance of risk-taking in business growth is vital for harnessing the power of innovation. It is about fostering a culture that encourages calculated risks, creativity, resilience, and adaptability. Embracing risk-taking as an essential component of the innovation process is a cornerstone of staying competitive and driving meaningful growth in today's ever-changing business landscape.

Failure is often viewed with apprehension and disappointment in the business world. However, when examined through a different lens, it becomes evident that failure can serve as a potent catalyst for creativity. Understanding how failures spark creative solutions sheds light on the transformative power of setbacks and missteps.

One of the ways in which failure fuels creativity is by challenging existing paradigms. When businesses encounter failure, they are compelled to reevaluate their approaches and question assumptions that may have led to the setback. This process of introspection and self-examination can lead to innovative solutions that break away from conventional thinking.

- Failures disrupt the status quo and force organizations to think differently. In the face of adversity, individuals and teams are often driven to explore new ideas and unconventional strategies to overcome challenges. The pressure and constraints imposed by failure can ignite a sense of urgency and creativity that might not have been present in a more comfortable environment.

- Failures also push individuals out of their comfort zones. When confronted with unexpected outcomes, employees and leaders are encouraged to adapt and explore alternative paths. This adaptability fosters a culture of flexibility and open-mindedness, key ingredients for creative problem-solving.

- Failure often leads to the discovery of previously uncharted territories. It forces businesses to explore new avenues, experiment with untested concepts, and take calculated risks. In this exploration, organizations may stumble upon innovative solutions, products, or services that they might not have otherwise considered.

The resilience developed through learning from failure is a driving force behind creative solutions. When businesses weather setbacks and emerge stronger, they build a foundation of confidence and determination that can lead to innovative thinking. This resilience allows organizations to persevere in the face of challenges and find creative ways to overcome them.

Lastly, failure provides valuable feedback. It offers insights into what does not work, which can be as instructive as knowing what does work. Armed with this feedback, businesses can refine their strategies and develop more creative and effective solutions.

Learning from failure is a powerful catalyst for creativity. It challenges conventional thinking, disrupts comfort zones, encourages adaptability, leads to the discovery of new territories, builds resilience, and provides invaluable feedback. When organizations embrace failure as a teacher rather than a foe, they unlock the potential for creative solutions that drive innovation and propel them forward in an ever-evolving business landscape.

Let's explore a couple of case studies showcasing how innovation can emerge from failure:

Apple Inc.: The Newton MessagePad and the Birth of the iPhone

The Newton MessagePad, introduced by Apple in the early 1990s, represented the company's pioneering attempt to create a personal digital assistant (PDA). This innovative device aimed to revolutionize how individuals managed their daily tasks and schedules, embodying Apple's forward-thinking approach to technology. Despite its groundbreaking potential, the Newton MessagePad encountered significant technical difficulties and failed to resonate with the market, leading to underwhelming sales and its eventual discontinuation. This setback, however, did not spell the end of Apple's ventures into portable devices.

The lessons learned from the Newton's shortcomings were invaluable. Apple meticulously analyzed the feedback and technical issues that plagued the Newton, using these insights to inform future product development. This period of reflection and recalibration was crucial for Apple, highlighting the importance of user experience and market readiness in the success of technology products.

Years later, Apple's introduction of the iPhone marked a stark contrast to the Newton's tale. With the iPhone, Apple successfully integrated multiple functionalities into a single device, offering consumers a phone, music player, camera, and internet browser, all with an intuitive user interface. The iPhone's launch in 2007 was met with critical acclaim and commercial success, dramatically altering the landscape of the smartphone industry and cementing Apple's reputation as an innovator.

The transition from the Newton MessagePad to the iPhone illustrates Apple's resilience and commitment to innovation. By embracing its past failures and learning from them, Apple managed to redefine the mobile computing space. The company's ability to pivot and adapt, guided by a deeper understanding of consumer needs and technological possibilities, played a pivotal role in the iPhone's success.

Apple's journey from the Newton's disappointment to the iPhone's triumph underscores the transformative power of failure. Instead of retreating, Apple leveraged its experiences with the Newton to push the boundaries of what was possible in mobile technology. This adaptive approach not only salvaged Apple's ambitions in the personal digital assistant space but also led to the creation of a product that would become a cultural icon and industry standard.

The evolution from the Newton MessagePad to the iPhone serves as a compelling case study in strategic resilience and innovation management. Apple's experience highlights the critical role of failure in the innovation process, demonstrating how setbacks can be converted into strategic opportunities for breakthrough success. Through this lens, the Newton MessagePad's legacy is not one of failure but a foundational step towards the development of revolutionary technology that would forever change the global tech landscape.

IBM: From PCjr to the IBM ThinkPad

In the early 1980s, IBM ventured into the burgeoning home computer market with the introduction of the PCjr. Designed to be an affordable and user-friendly option for consumers, the PCjr aimed to extend IBM's dominance from the business sector into personal computing. Despite its potential, the PCjr was met with a lukewarm reception, primarily due to its technical limitations and high-cost relative to its capabilities. The product struggled to compete with other home computers of the time, leading to disappointing sales figures and its eventual discontinuation. This experience, while initially a setback, provided IBM with valuable insights into the consumer market.

Undeterred by the failure of the PCjr, IBM took the lessons learned from this endeavor to heart. The company recognized the importance of not only meeting but exceeding consumer expectations in terms of performance, reliability, and value for money. This reflection period was crucial for IBM as it recalibrated its strategy in the personal computing space. The insights gained from the PCjr's shortcomings influenced IBM's approach to product development, pushing the company to prioritize innovation and user experience in its future offerings.

In the 1990s, IBM introduced the ThinkPad, a line of laptop computers that marked a significant departure from the PCjr's legacy. The ThinkPad was engineered with the needs of professional and business users in mind, featuring a robust build, innovative design elements, and cutting-edge technology for its time. Notably, the ThinkPad was among the first to introduce features such as the TrackPoint pointing device and a butterfly keyboard in some models, which were hailed as revolutionary. The ThinkPad's success was immediate and profound, quickly becoming the laptop of choice for businesses and consumers alike and setting a new standard for what was expected in a laptop computer.

The ThinkPad's acclaim and commercial success represented a redemption of sorts for IBM, showcasing the company's resilience and capacity for innovation. It highlighted IBM's ability to pivot and adapt its strategy based on previous experiences. The ThinkPad became synonymous with quality and reliability in the laptop market, contributing significantly to IBM's reputation and success in the computer hardware industry. This shift not only solidified IBM's place in the personal computing landscape but also demonstrated the strategic value of learning from past failures to achieve future successes.

IBM's journey from the PCjr to the ThinkPad is a testament to the power of resilience, strategic adaptation, and the pursuit of excellence in technology. It serves as an inspiring case study for businesses and innovators, illustrating that setbacks can be transformed into stepping stones towards groundbreaking achievements. By embracing the lessons from the PCjr and committing to innovation and quality, IBM was able to redefine its legacy in the personal computing market with the ThinkPad, paving the way for decades of influence and leadership in technology.

IBM's transition from the unsuccessful PCjr to the highly successful ThinkPad exemplifies the importance of learning from failure, understanding market needs, and relentlessly pursuing innovation. This story underscores the potential for organizations to overcome challenges, adapt strategies, and ultimately achieve remarkable turnarounds through perseverance and strategic thinking. The ThinkPad's legacy, rooted in the lessons of the PCjr, continues to influence the design and development of personal computing devices, reflecting IBM's enduring impact on the technology industry.

These case studies illustrate how companies can leverage failure as a steppingstone to innovation. By analyzing what went wrong, adjusting their strategies, and pursuing new opportunities, organizations can transform setbacks into catalysts for groundbreaking advancements and enduring success.

Building an innovative culture within an organization, especially after experiencing setbacks or failures, is a challenging but vital endeavor. Such a culture empowers employees to think creatively, take calculated risks, and contribute to the continuous improvement of the business. Here are key strategies for fostering an innovative culture post-failure:

1. Leadership Commitment: Leaders must demonstrate a commitment to innovation and create a safe space for experimentation. Their actions and attitudes set the tone for the entire organization. When leaders openly acknowledge failures as learning opportunities and embrace innovative thinking, it encourages others to do the same.

2. Learning from Failure: Encourage a culture of learning from failures. When setbacks occur, rather than assigning blame, focus on understanding what went wrong and how

to prevent it in the future. Share these lessons transparently with the organization to promote a culture of continuous improvement.

3. Clear Vision and Values: Define a clear vision and set of values that prioritize innovation. Make it known that innovation aligns with the organization's core mission and is integral to its success. Employees should understand how their work contributes to the overall innovation goals.

4. Open Communication: Create channels for open and honest communication. Encourage employees to share their ideas and concerns without fear of reprisal. Regularly solicit feedback from all levels of the organization and act on it when possible.

5. Diverse Teams: Foster diversity in teams, as it brings a variety of perspectives and ideas to the table. Different backgrounds, experiences, and viewpoints often lead to more innovative solutions. Encourage collaboration among cross-functional teams to promote diversity of thought.

6. Resources for Innovation: Allocate resources specifically for innovation initiatives. This includes budgetary support, dedicated time for brainstorming and experimentation, and access to relevant training and tools.

7. Recognition and Rewards: Implement recognition and reward systems that celebrate and reinforce innovative behaviors and outcomes. This can include acknowledging employees who propose innovative ideas or contribute to successful innovations.

8. Tolerance for Risk: Cultivate a culture that accepts calculated risks. Employees should feel encouraged to take chances on new ideas and initiatives, knowing that not every endeavor will succeed but that failure is seen as a steppingstone to eventual success.

9. Innovation Champions: Identify and empower innovation champions within the organization. These individuals can help drive the innovation agenda, inspire others, and serve as role models for creative thinking.

10. Continuous Improvement: Encourage a mindset of continuous improvement, not only in products and services but also in processes and operations. Encourage employees to seek efficiencies and improvements in their daily work.

11. Training and Development: Invest in ongoing training and development programs that enhance creative and innovative thinking. These programs can include workshops on design thinking, problem-solving, and ideation.

12. Metrics and Measurement: Establish key performance indicators (KPIs) to measure innovation success. Regularly evaluate and adjust innovation efforts based on these metrics to ensure they align with business goals.

By implementing these strategies, organizations can cultivate an innovative culture that thrives even in the face of setbacks. Such a culture not only encourages employees to embrace innovation but also positions the organization to adapt, evolve, and ultimately succeed in a rapidly changing business landscape.

A Variety of Tools and Methodologies for Innovating through Failures:

Root Cause Analysis: When faced with a failure, it's essential to understand why it occurred. Root cause analysis tools like the "5 Whys" technique or Fishbone diagrams (Ishikawa diagrams) help organizations dig deep to identify the underlying causes. By asking "why" multiple times or visualizing the potential causes, teams can pinpoint the root issues that led to the failure. This understanding forms the basis for targeted and effective solutions.

SWOT Analysis: A SWOT analysis examines an organization's internal strengths and weaknesses, along with external opportunities and threats. It's a valuable tool for post-failure innovation. By assessing these factors, organizations can identify areas where innovation is needed to capitalize on opportunities or address weaknesses. This structured analysis guides strategic decisions and innovation initiatives.

Design Thinking: Design thinking is a human-centered approach to innovation that encourages empathy, ideation, and rapid prototyping. It involves multidisciplinary teams brainstorming and co-creating innovative solutions while considering the end-user's perspective. This methodology fosters a creative and user-centric mindset, making it effective in generating innovative ideas post-failure.

Brainstorming and Ideation: Creativity is at the heart of innovation, and brainstorming sessions are a common method to stimulate creative thinking. Techniques like brainstorming boards, mind mapping, or SCAMPER (Substitute, Combine, Adapt, Modify, Put to another use, Eliminate, Reverse) help teams generate a wide range of ideas and solutions. These sessions provide a structured environment for idea generation and problem-solving.

Prototyping and Rapid Testing: To bring innovative ideas to life, organizations often use prototyping and rapid testing. Prototyping involves creating tangible representations of concepts or minimum viable products (MVPs) for quick testing and validation. Tools like 3D printing, wireframing software, or rapid development platforms aid in the creation of prototypes, allowing teams to experiment and iterate efficiently.

Innovation Labs and Incubators: Establishing dedicated innovation labs or incubators within an organization provides a space for nurturing creative ideas and projects. These labs offer resources, mentorship, and a supportive environment for experimentation and development of innovative solutions post-failure.

Open Innovation Platforms: Collaborating with external partners, such as startups or research institutions, through open innovation platforms is a strategy to access fresh perspectives and expertise. These platforms facilitate idea exchange, joint projects, and access to external resources, enriching the innovation process.

Technology Scanning: Staying informed about emerging technologies and industry trends is crucial for identifying opportunities for technological innovation. Technology scanning tools help organizations track new developments, enabling them to leverage cutting-edge solutions to address past failures and enhance their competitiveness.

Failure Mode and Effects Analysis (FMEA): FMEA is a systematic tool for evaluating potential failure modes of a process or product and their consequences. It helps prioritize areas for improvement and innovation by identifying critical points where intervention can prevent future failures.

Voice of the Customer (VoC): To ensure customer-centric innovation, collecting feedback directly from customers is essential. Methods like surveys, focus groups, or interviews provide insights into customer needs, pain points, and preferences. Incorporating the voice of the customer into post-failure innovation efforts helps align solutions with real-world demands.

Agile and Lean Principles: Embracing agile and lean methodologies encourages iterative development, continuous improvement, and responsiveness to customer feedback. These principles foster a culture of innovation by promoting adaptability and collaboration, enabling organizations to pivot effectively after a failure.

Scalable Innovation Frameworks: Frameworks like the Three Horizons Model categorize innovation efforts into short-term, mid-term, and long-term initiatives. This approach ensures a balanced innovation portfolio that addresses immediate challenges while also paving the way for future growth and transformation.

Innovation Management Software: Innovation management software platforms streamline the innovation process by facilitating idea submission, collaboration, and project tracking. These tools help capture, evaluate, and implement innovative ideas effectively, ensuring that innovation efforts are organized and aligned with strategic objectives.

Crowdsourcing: To tap into a diverse pool of ideas and expertise, organizations can leverage crowdsourcing. Crowdsourcing platforms allow employees or external communities to contribute innovative ideas and solutions. This collective intelligence approach can be particularly valuable in generating creative responses to setbacks.

Metrics and Key Performance Indicators (KPIs): Establishing clear KPIs is essential for measuring the success and impact of innovation efforts post-failure. Regularly assessing these metrics allows organizations to evaluate the effectiveness of their innovation strategies and make informed adjustments to ensure alignment with overall business goals.

By leveraging these tools and methodologies, organizations can systematically approach innovation after experiencing setbacks or failures. This structured approach fosters a culture of creativity, resilience, and continuous improvement, enabling organizations to harness failures as opportunities for growth and positive transformation.

In this chapter, we explored the pivotal role of failure in driving innovation and future business success. We began by understanding how failure can serve as a catalyst for creativity, challenging conventional thinking, and encouraging organizations to explore new ideas and unconventional approaches. Failure's disruptive nature forces individuals and teams to think differently, fostering a culture of flexibility and open-mindedness.

We also discussed various tools and methodologies that organizations can employ to innovate after setbacks. These tools, ranging from root cause analysis to innovation management software, provide structured approaches for generating creative solutions and improving processes.

We examined the importance of fostering an innovative culture post-failure, emphasizing leadership commitment, learning from failures, clear vision and values, open communication, and a tolerance for risk as key elements in cultivating an environment that encourages innovation. The chapter highlighted case studies of successful companies that innovated after experiencing failure, illustrating how setbacks can be transformed into stepping stones toward groundbreaking advancements.

The journey through this chapter underscores a fundamental truth in the world of business: failure is not a dead end but a critical junction on the path to innovation and future success. By embracing failures as learning experiences, organizations can challenge the status quo, adapt, and transform setbacks into catalysts for creativity.

Innovation post-failure is not a solitary endeavor but a structured and collaborative process. It relies on tools, methodologies, and a culture that encourages creativity, resilience, and adaptability. Through this process, organizations can harness the power of setbacks to not only recover but to thrive in a rapidly changing business landscape.

Innovation is not just a response to failure; it is a mindset that fosters growth, competitiveness, and sustainability. By acknowledging the role of failure in sparking innovation and by leveraging it as a source of inspiration, businesses can position themselves to navigate uncertainty, seize opportunities, and embark on a path of continuous improvement. In doing so, they embrace the transformative power of failure on the journey toward future success.

Chapter 7: Ethical Considerations and Integrity

In the complex landscape of business, ethical considerations and integrity are essential pillars that guide organizations through both triumphs and tribulations. This chapter delves into the profound importance of ethics and integrity in handling business failures. It is a journey that begins by defining ethical leadership within the context of setbacks, understanding what integrity truly means when confronted with adversity.

Challenges arise when business failures occur, often testing the ethical fabric of individuals and organizations. These challenges lead us to explore the common ethical dilemmas that surface post-failure, shedding light on the complexities faced by leaders and decision-makers.

But this chapter is not just about identifying challenges; it is about equipping leaders with the tools and strategies to make ethical decisions during tough times. We will delve into practical guidelines for ethical decision-making after failures, offering a compass to navigate the turbulent ethical waters that may arise.

To anchor our exploration, we will draw upon real-life case studies that showcase integrity in action. These examples will illuminate the ethical challenges faced by companies and how they resolved them, providing invaluable lessons for organizations striving to uphold their ethical principles in times of crisis.

Ultimately, this chapter aims to go beyond theory, offering tangible tools and frameworks to develop an ethical response framework. It is a guide for organizations seeking to foster ethical responses to failure, ensuring that their actions align with their values and principles.

Ethics and integrity are not optional in the face of business failures but are rather the foundation upon which ethical leaders and resilient organizations are built. This chapter will underscore the indispensable role of ethics in business failure management, emphasizing that ethical conduct is not only a moral imperative but a strategic one, critical for long-term success and sustainability.

In the realm of business, the significance of ethics and integrity becomes especially pronounced when navigating the treacherous waters of failure. While success can often shine a favorable light on an organization's ethics, it is in times of crisis and adversity that the true measure of ethical leadership is taken. This section delves into the critical role of ethics and integrity in the context of business failures.

Ethics and integrity are the moral compass that guides individuals and organizations through the complexities of the business world. They are the principles and values that shape decision-making, define corporate culture, and determine the actions taken when faced with challenges. In the context of failure, the importance of ethical conduct becomes even more pronounced.

When businesses encounter setbacks or failures, the ethical choices made in response can have far-reaching consequences. Decisions that prioritize short-term gains at the expense of long-term integrity can erode trust, tarnish reputations, and lead to irreparable damage. Conversely, ethical decisions can not only mitigate the impact of failure but also foster trust, loyalty, and resilience.

Ethical leadership in times of failure means adhering to principles such as transparency, accountability, and responsibility. It involves acknowledging mistakes, learning from them, and taking actions that prioritize the interests of stakeholders, including employees, customers, shareholders, and the broader community.

Furthermore, integrity is defined not only by how organizations handle their failures but also by their commitment to rectify the issues that led to those failures. It is about taking corrective actions, making amends, and implementing safeguards to prevent similar mistakes in the future.

In a world where information travels quickly, where reputation is paramount, and where ethical lapses can lead to severe legal and financial consequences, maintaining ethics and integrity is not just a moral imperative; it is a strategic necessity. Organizations that prioritize ethical conduct during and after failure demonstrate resilience, authenticity, and a commitment to long-term success.

Ethical leadership takes on a heightened significance when organizations grapple with failure. In such moments, leaders are called upon to navigate treacherous terrain, make challenging decisions, and uphold the principles of integrity even as the ground shakes beneath them. This section delves into the essence of ethical leadership in the context of failure and seeks to provide clarity on what integrity truly means when confronted with setbacks.

At its core, ethical leadership involves a steadfast commitment to moral principles, even in the face of adversity. It means staying true to one's values, maintaining transparency, and acting with honesty and fairness. However, in the context of failure, ethical leadership takes on specific characteristics and responsibilities.

Firstly, ethical leadership entails accountability. Leaders must take ownership of the failures that occur under their watch. They must be willing to acknowledge mistakes, accept responsibility, and be transparent about the causes of failure. This accountability is the foundation upon which trust can be rebuilt.

Secondly, ethical leadership involves empathy and consideration for stakeholders. When failure strikes, leaders must recognize the impact on employees, customers, shareholders, and the community at large. Ethical leaders prioritize the well-being of these stakeholders and strive to mitigate harm while seeking constructive solutions.

Thirdly, ethical leaders exhibit resilience. In the face of failure, they do not waver in their commitment to ethical principles. They understand that setbacks do not justify compromising on integrity, and they inspire their teams to uphold these values even during difficult times.

Ethical leadership is about learning and improvement. Leaders must view failure as an opportunity for growth, not just for themselves but for the entire organization. They engage in introspection, identify areas for improvement, and implement measures to prevent similar failures in the future.

Integrity in the face of setbacks means unwavering adherence to ethical principles, even when the path forward is uncertain. It means leading by example, demonstrating accountability, prioritizing stakeholders' interests, and using failures as stepping stones toward a more ethical and resilient future.

When organizations face failure, they often encounter a range of ethical dilemmas that can test the very core of their values and integrity. This section explores some of the common ethical challenges that arise in the aftermath of setbacks, shedding light on the complexities faced by leaders and decision-makers.

- Transparency vs. Protecting Reputation: One of the first ethical dilemmas centers on the balance between transparency and protecting the organization's reputation. Leaders must decide how much information to disclose about the failure. While transparency is essential for rebuilding trust, sharing too much too soon can have adverse consequences on the organization's image and stakeholders' confidence.

- Accountability vs. Blame: Another challenge lies in distinguishing between holding individuals accountable for their actions and assigning blame. Ethical leaders seek to identify responsible parties without resorting to scapegoating, recognizing that fostering a culture of accountability is more productive than assigning blame.

- Conflicts of Interest: Failure situations can reveal conflicts of interest among leaders or decision-makers. Ethical leaders must navigate these conflicts impartially, ensuring that personal interests do not compromise the organization's best interests.

- Ethical Decision-Making vs. Financial Pressures: Financial pressures often mount during failure scenarios, leading to ethical dilemmas related to cost-cutting measures, layoffs, or financial reporting. Leaders must resist the temptation to compromise ethical standards in pursuit of short-term financial relief.

- Loyalty to Stakeholders: Balancing loyalty to various stakeholders, including employees, shareholders, and customers, can be challenging. Ethical leaders must prioritize the interests of all stakeholders, avoiding favoritism and making decisions that benefit the broader community.

- Whistleblower Concerns: In some cases, employees or insiders may have knowledge of unethical or illegal practices that contributed to the failure. Ethical leaders must create a safe environment for whistleblowers to come forward and address these concerns without fear of retaliation.

- Regulatory Compliance: Navigating regulatory compliance during failure situations can be complex. Leaders must make ethical choices that ensure compliance while upholding the organization's integrity and reputation.

- Long-Term vs. Short-Term Goals: Ethical dilemmas often arise when leaders must choose between actions that provide immediate relief or those that align with long-term goals and values. Maintaining integrity during failures requires prioritizing long-term sustainability over short-term gains.

- Communication and Honesty: Deciding what information to communicate to stakeholders and how to do so with honesty and empathy is an ongoing challenge. Leaders must be careful not to mislead or create false expectations, as such actions can erode trust further.

- Rebuilding Trust: Restoring trust after a failure can be a daunting task. Ethical leaders must navigate the delicate process of rebuilding trust through consistent actions, transparency, and demonstrated commitment to ethical conduct.

Identifying and addressing these common ethical dilemmas is crucial for leaders and organizations seeking to maintain integrity during and after failures. It highlights the complexity of ethical decision-making in the face of adversity and underscores the need for thoughtful, principled leadership to guide organizations toward ethical responses and, ultimately, recovery.

In the challenging aftermath of business failures, the process of ethical decision-making becomes paramount. Leaders and decision-makers must adhere to a structured approach that prioritizes moral principles and values. A foundational step in this process is reflecting upon the core values of the organization. A thorough understanding of these values and principles serves as the compass that guides ethical choices. When ethical dilemmas arise, referencing these values can provide clarity and guidance.

Another crucial strategy is to consult established ethical frameworks and models, such as utilitarianism, deontology, and virtue ethics. These frameworks offer different perspectives on ethical dilemmas and help analyze and weigh the moral consequences of decisions. Seeking diverse perspectives through open and inclusive discussions within the organization is equally important. Gathering input from various stakeholders, including employees, board members, and external advisors, can reveal different viewpoints and shed light on ethical dimensions that may not be immediately apparent.

Long-term thinking is a hallmark of ethical decision-making. Leaders must assess how their choices will impact the organization's reputation, stakeholder trust, and sustainability in the years to come. Prioritizing stakeholder interests is a fundamental principle of ethical leadership. This involves considering how decisions will affect all stakeholders, including employees, customers, shareholders, and the broader community, and striving for outcomes that benefit the greater good.

Transparency in communication and accountability for actions are essential components of ethical decision-making. Leaders should be forthright about the situation, acknowledge mistakes, and outline the steps being taken to rectify the failure and prevent future occurrences. Additionally, ensuring that decisions align with legal and regulatory requirements is paramount. Ethical choices should not compromise compliance with applicable laws and regulations, and seeking legal counsel when necessary is advisable.

In larger organizations, consulting ethical committees or advisors can provide valuable guidance on complex ethical dilemmas. Leveraging their expertise can help ensure ethical decision-making. Ethical leaders also consider conducting ethical risk assessments to proactively identify potential challenges and dilemmas that may arise in the wake of failures, allowing for better preparation and ethical decision-making when these challenges materialize.

Learning from ethical role models both within and outside the organization can provide valuable insights. Studying the decisions and actions of leaders known for their ethical conduct can serve as a source of inspiration and guidance. Investing in ongoing ethical training and education for the team is another valuable strategy. Providing them with the knowledge and tools to make ethical decisions reinforces a culture of ethics and integrity within the organization.

After making an ethical decision, the process continues with reflection on its implications and outcomes. Ethical leaders embrace a mindset of continuous improvement, learning from both successes and failures to refine their ethical decision-making processes. In the turbulent aftermath of failure, ethical decision-making becomes a beacon of integrity that guides organizations toward recovery and growth, ultimately upholding ethical values even during tough times.

Let's delve into real-life case studies that exemplify integrity in action in the face of ethical challenges and resolutions during business failures.

Case Study 1: Enron Corporation

Enron Corporation, once considered a giant in the energy industry, faced a catastrophic failure in the early 2000s. The company's unethical financial practices and accounting fraud came to light, leading to one of the most significant corporate scandals in history.

Ethical Challenge: The primary ethical challenge was the deliberate manipulation of financial statements and the concealment of massive debt, all while promoting an image of financial stability and growth to shareholders and the public.

Resolution: Following the scandal's exposure, Enron's leadership faced severe legal consequences, including convictions and imprisonment. The company filed for bankruptcy, and a rigorous investigation led to regulatory reforms, including the Sarbanes-Oxley Act. This legislation aimed to enhance corporate governance, transparency, and ethical conduct in the business world.

Case Study 2: Johnson & Johnson's Tylenol Crisis

In 1982, Johnson & Johnson faced a significant ethical crisis when cyanide-laced Tylenol capsules led to multiple deaths in the Chicago area.

Ethical Challenge: The challenge was the potential impact on public safety and trust in the pharmaceutical industry. Johnson &

Johnson needed to act swiftly and ethically to protect consumers and regain trust.

Resolution: Johnson & Johnson demonstrated exceptional ethical leadership by immediately recalling over 31 million bottles of Tylenol, even though they were not responsible for the tampering. The company prioritized consumer safety over financial losses, costing them millions. They implemented tamper-evident packaging and worked closely with law enforcement to identify and bring the perpetrator to justice. This case remains a testament to the company's commitment to ethical conduct and customer safety.

Case Study 3: Toyota's Unintended Acceleration Crisis

Toyota faced a significant ethical and public relations crisis in the late 2000s when reports of unintended acceleration in its vehicles surfaced.

Ethical Challenge: The challenge was to address safety concerns promptly and ethically while maintaining the company's reputation for quality and safety.

Resolution: Toyota responded by issuing recalls, halting production, and cooperating with government investigations. The company acknowledged the problem, took full responsibility, and worked to rectify it swiftly. This approach, focused on customer safety and transparency, demonstrated a commitment to ethical conduct. Toyota implemented extensive quality control measures to prevent future issues and rebuild trust with its customers.

These case studies illustrate the importance of ethical leadership and integrity in times of crisis and failure. Enron's ethical lapse led to severe consequences, while Johnson & Johnson and Toyota's ethical responses enabled them to recover trust and maintain their long-term success. These examples underscore that ethical choices made during business failures can have lasting impacts on an organization's reputation, resilience, and ultimate success.

Developing an Ethical Response Framework entails the integration of various tools and frameworks to facilitate ethical responses to failures within organizations. These elements provide a structured approach to guide decision-makers when faced with challenging ethical dilemmas.

Incorporating ethical decision-making models into organizational processes is essential for ensuring decisions align with core ethical principles. The "Four-Component Model" and the "Ethical Decision-Making Framework" are pivotal in guiding individuals and organizations through the complexities of ethical dilemmas. These models facilitate a step-by-step analysis, beginning with the identification of ethical issues, assessment of the situation from multiple ethical perspectives, decision-making based on ethical grounds, and culminating in the implementation of actions that uphold ethical standards.

Such models emphasize the importance of ethical sensitivity, judgment, motivation, and character. By systematically applying these components, organizations can navigate ethical challenges with clarity and integrity. This approach not only aids in resolving immediate dilemmas but also contributes to the development of a robust ethical culture within the organization. It ensures that ethical considerations are not peripheral but integral to the decision-making process, reflecting the organization's commitment to ethical practices.

The structured nature of these models offers a clear framework for evaluating options and consequences, encouraging a thorough consideration of all stakeholders affected by the decision. This comprehensive evaluation helps in minimizing harm and maximizing benefits, leading to outcomes that are justifiable and ethically sound. By fostering an environment where ethical deliberation is standard practice, organizations can build trust and credibility among employees, customers, and the wider community.

Implementing these ethical decision-making models serves as a proactive measure against potential ethical breaches. It equips individuals with the tools and mindset needed to preemptively identify and address ethical issues before they escalate into larger problems. This proactive stance on ethics can significantly reduce risks and safeguard the organization's reputation.

The integration of established ethical decision-making models into organizational frameworks is a critical strategy for promoting ethical integrity. It ensures that decisions are made with a principled approach, fostering a culture of transparency and accountability. By prioritizing ethics in decision-making, organizations not only navigate dilemmas more effectively but also enhance their ethical standing and resilience in the face of challenges.

To further support ethical responses, organizations can establish ethics committees or engage ethical advisors. These experts can offer valuable insights and recommendations on complex ethical matters, providing guidance to decision-makers as they navigate challenging decisions. Their expertise helps ensure that ethical principles are upheld during crises and failures.

Ethical impact assessment tools are essential within the framework to evaluate the potential ethical consequences of decisions. Such tools enable organizations to identify risks and benefits associated with various courses of action, helping decision-makers make informed and ethical choices that align with the organization's values.

Stakeholder engagement frameworks are crucial for involving key stakeholders, including employees, customers, shareholders, and the broader community, in decision-making processes. Encouraging diverse perspectives and considering the interests of all stakeholders is a fundamental aspect of ethical responses to failures.

Ethical risk management is another vital element within the framework, allowing organizations to proactively identify and assess ethical risks associated with different actions or strategies. By addressing potential ethical challenges before they escalate, organizations can mitigate the impact of failures on their ethical reputation.

Investing in ongoing ethical training and education programs for employees at all levels reinforces a culture of ethics and integrity within the organization. These programs focus on ethical decision-making, recognizing ethical dilemmas, and ensuring that employees understand and embody the organization's ethical principles.

To monitor and assess adherence to ethical standards, organizations can conduct regular ethical audits and monitoring processes. These assessments encompass reviews of decisions, actions, and behaviors, helping identify areas for improvement in ethical responses and conduct.

Establishing confidential and anonymous reporting systems, such as ethics hotlines or reporting portals, empowers employees to report ethical violations without fear of retaliation. These systems encourage transparency and accountability while enabling organizations to address ethical concerns promptly.

Investing in the development of ethical leadership skills among managers and executives is critical. Ethical leaders set the tone for the organization and serve as role models for ethical behavior, reinforcing the importance of ethics and integrity within the workplace.

Clear and ethical crisis communication protocols are essential to guide how organizations communicate with stakeholders during failures or crises. Prioritizing transparency, honesty, and empathy in communication helps maintain trust and integrity in challenging times.

Conducting post-failure ethical analyses is a crucial step in the framework. These analyses evaluate how ethical principles were upheld or compromised during the crisis, allowing organizations to learn from their experiences and identify areas for improvement in ethical responses to future failures.

By integrating these elements into an Ethical Response Framework, organizations can cultivate a culture of ethics and integrity that guides decision-making, prevents ethical lapses, enhances reputation, and ensures long-term resilience and success, even in the face of failure.

In this chapter, we have explored the pivotal role of ethics in the context of business failure management. The journey through various aspects of ethical considerations in the face of setbacks has illuminated the significance of prioritizing moral principles and values when navigating challenging times.

Ethics, as we have witnessed, serves as a beacon of guidance when organizations confront failure. It encompasses a commitment to transparency, accountability, and responsibility, even in the midst of adversity. Ethical leaders acknowledge their mistakes, learn from them, and take actions that prioritize the interests of stakeholders, fostering trust, loyalty, and resilience.

Defining ethical leadership in failure contexts revealed that ethical leaders are not only accountable for their actions but also empathetic and considerate of stakeholders' well-being. They exhibit resilience and view failure as an opportunity for growth, committing to rectify past errors and prevent their recurrence.

Challenges to maintaining integrity during failures exposed the complex ethical dilemmas that organizations can face. These dilemmas include balancing transparency and reputation protection, distinguishing accountability from blame, managing conflicts of interest, and resisting the temptation to compromise ethical standards under financial pressures.

Strategies for ethical decision-making after failures outlined a structured approach that encourages reflection on core values, consultation of ethical frameworks, and the inclusion of diverse perspectives. Long-term impacts, stakeholder interests, transparency, accountability, and legal compliance were prioritized in the decision-making process.

We delved into the practical tools and frameworks that constitute an Ethical Response Framework. These tools include ethical decision-making models, codes of ethics, ethics committees, ethical impact assessments, stakeholder engagement frameworks, ethical risk management, ethical training, and ethical audits, among others. These tools collectively support a culture of ethics and integrity within organizations, guiding decision-makers in making principled choices during challenging times.

The case studies illustrated how organizations can respond to ethical challenges and crises with integrity. Enron's downfall showcased the consequences of ethical lapses, while Johnson & Johnson's Tylenol crisis and Toyota's unintended acceleration crisis demonstrated the power of ethical responses in restoring trust and reputation.

In summary, ethics is not an abstract concept but a tangible and essential aspect of leadership and organizational culture, especially when confronted with adversity and failure. It serves as the compass that guides organizations toward ethical responses, recovery, and long-term success. By embracing ethical principles and integrating them into decision-making processes, organizations can navigate the turbulent waters of failure with integrity, resilience, and a commitment to the greater good of all stakeholders. In doing so, they not only manage failure but also emerge stronger and more ethically robust.

Chapter 8: Personal and Professional Growth from Failure

In Chapter 8, we embark on a profound exploration of how failure, often viewed as a stumbling block, can be transformed into a stepping stone for personal and professional growth. As we journey through this chapter, we will uncover the intricate and interconnected relationship between personal and professional development, discovering how one influences the other in profound ways.

At the heart of this discussion is the recognition that failure is not merely a setback in our careers or endeavors; it is an opportunity for holistic growth that transcends professional boundaries. We will delve into the powerful intersection of personal and professional development, where lessons learned from failure have the potential to reshape not only our careers but also our lives.

Our exploration begins by understanding how personal growth plays a pivotal role in professional success. We will explore the ways in which the lessons learned from failures shape our character, resilience, and capacity for empathy. Failure becomes a transformative teacher, offering us insights that extend far beyond the boardroom.

Learning empathy through failure emerges as a central theme, as we explore how setbacks can enhance our understanding of the human experience. We will witness how empathy, cultivated through adversity, becomes a powerful tool for building and strengthening relationships, both in our professional and personal lives.

As we navigate through this chapter, we will also provide guidance on reassessing and setting new priorities after experiencing failure. The process of reevaluating our aspirations and objectives can be a crucial step towards achieving alignment between our personal and professional pursuits.

We will explore strategies for maintaining balance in the wake of failure, recognizing that the pursuit of professional success should not come at the expense of our well-being and personal lives. Achieving equilibrium becomes essential as we harness the lessons learned from failure to fuel our growth.

This chapter will sum up the profound transformations that can occur when we embrace failure not as an obstacle but as a catalyst for holistic growth. We will emphasize the interconnected nature of personal and professional development and how these facets of our lives can flourish when we navigate the challenging terrain of failure with resilience and open hearts. Through this exploration, we aim to inspire readers to harness the transformative power of failure, ultimately leading them towards a more fulfilling and balanced existence, both personally and professionally.

Failure is often perceived as an unwelcome companion on our journey through life, a force that obstructs progress and challenges our aspirations. However, in this chapter, we will explore a different perspective—one that views failure not as an endpoint but as a powerful catalyst for personal and professional growth.

Failure, when embraced with the right mindset, can serve as a fertile ground for profound transformation. It offers us an invaluable opportunity to reevaluate our paths, refine our skills, and emerge stronger and wiser. As we delve into this overview, we will uncover the multifaceted ways in which failure can lead to growth, both in our personal lives and in our professional endeavors.

- Resilience and Adaptability: One of the most immediate and tangible outcomes of failure is the cultivation of resilience. When we face setbacks and disappointments, we are compelled to confront adversity head-on. This process strengthens our resilience, enabling us to bounce back from challenges with newfound determination and adaptability. These qualities are not confined to professional success but extend to our personal lives, helping us navigate life's ups and downs with grace and fortitude.

- Self-Discovery: Failure often forces us to engage in introspection and self-discovery. As we analyze the reasons behind our setbacks, we gain a deeper understanding of our strengths, weaknesses, and areas for improvement. This self-awareness becomes a cornerstone of personal growth, guiding us towards self-fulfillment and authenticity.

- Character Development: The crucible of failure has the power to shape our character in profound ways. It tests our values, integrity, and determination. We are challenged to uphold our principles and ethics even when faced with adversity. This process of character development extends its influence to our professional lives, where integrity and ethical conduct are essential components of success.

- Learning and Innovation: Failure is a potent teacher, offering valuable lessons that propel us towards innovation and growth. It encourages us to think critically, identify areas for improvement, and adapt our strategies. This approach to learning extends beyond professional settings, enabling us to embrace a growth mindset in our personal development.

- Empathy and Interpersonal Skills: The experience of failure fosters empathy—an understanding of the human condition, its struggles, and vulnerabilities. This heightened empathetic awareness enhances our interpersonal skills, making us more compassionate and effective communicators. These qualities are not only essential for professional success but also for nurturing meaningful relationships in our personal lives.

- New Opportunities and Resilient Goals: Failure often redirects our paths, leading us towards new opportunities and more resilient goals. It challenges us to reassess our priorities and align our ambitions with our authentic selves. This process of goal realignment applies equally to personal and professional pursuits.

- Balance and Well-Being: Lastly, failure reminds us of the importance of balance and well-being in our lives. It encourages us to prioritize self-care, mental health, and personal fulfillment. These priorities, when incorporated into our professional lives, foster a holistic approach to success that encompasses both personal and professional growth.

This overview underscores that failure is not a dead-end but a transformative crossroads. It offers us the chance to cultivate resilience, deepen self-awareness, and refine our character. These outcomes resonate not only in our professional achievements but also in our personal lives, where authenticity, empathy, and a sense of purpose become the cornerstones of meaningful growth. As we continue our exploration, we will delve into these facets in more detail, uncovering the profound synergy between personal and professional development that emerges from the crucible of failure.

We now delve into the symbiotic relationship between personal and professional development, emphasizing how personal growth exerts a profound influence on one's professional achievements. Personal development is not confined to isolated self-improvement endeavors; rather, it extends its reach into the professional sphere, contributing substantially to success in one's career and occupational life.

Firstly, personal growth nurtures self-confidence, a cornerstone of professional success. As individuals gain deeper insights into themselves and their capabilities, their self-assuredness grows. This enhanced self-confidence empowers them to embrace challenges, lead teams, and make resolute decisions in their professional roles.

Secondly, personal development equips individuals with resilience, a critical asset in navigating professional setbacks and adversities. It fortifies them to rebound from failures, adapt to evolving circumstances, and maintain composure during high-stress scenarios—attributes indispensable for professional advancement.

Effective communication skills, an essential ingredient for professional triumph, stem from personal growth. Heightened self-awareness and interpersonal acumen enable individuals to articulate ideas, negotiate effectively, and collaborate harmoniously with colleagues, clients, and stakeholders in the workplace.

Personal development fosters emotional intelligence, an invaluable asset in professional settings. Mastery of emotional self-regulation and the ability to empathize with others enhance leadership effectiveness, teamwork, and adept conflict resolution—integral components of professional achievement.

Leadership capabilities also flourish through personal growth. As individuals gain deeper insights into their values and beliefs, they evolve into authentic leaders. Authentic leadership garners respect and inspires trust and loyalty among team members, fostering professional accomplishment. Personal development nurtures adaptability and a growth-oriented mindset, pivotal attributes in a rapidly evolving professional landscape. The capacity to learn, adapt, and confront novel challenges positions individuals for career progression.

Building upon interpersonal skills, personal growth emphasizes effective networking and relationship building. Robust professional relationships, whether with peers, mentors, or industry connections, fuel career advancement and provide opportunities for growth.

Goal setting and motivation receive a significant boost through personal development. The ability to define meaningful objectives and sustain motivation is a fundamental aspect of professional success, propelling individuals toward their career aspirations.

Equally vital are time management and productivity skills, honed during personal development. In the professional arena, efficient workload management, meeting deadlines, and task execution are instrumental for success. Personal growth enhances conflict resolution proficiencies, a crucial skill in professional environments where disagreements are inevitable. Proficient conflict resolution fosters harmonious workplace dynamics.

The confluence of personal and professional development enriches the qualities and competencies pivotal for career success. Personal growth amplifies self-confidence, resilience, communication, emotional intelligence, leadership, adaptability, networking, goal setting, time management, and conflict resolution—essentially empowering individuals for prosperous professional journeys. As we delve deeper into the interconnected nature of personal and professional growth, we will unravel how this synergy can lead to a more gratifying and thriving professional voyage.

Failure, as a teacher of resilience and adaptability, also deepens our ability to empathize with others. It provides a unique opportunity to broaden our empathetic horizons through the complex emotions associated with setbacks.

Through our own experiences of failure, we gain a humbling recognition of our vulnerabilities. This realization fosters a sense of shared humanity, making it easier to empathize with others facing similar challenges. We become attuned to the struggles and hardships that others may be enduring, as we can relate to feelings of frustration, disappointment, and uncertainty.

Setbacks often involve facing criticism, judgment, or rejection, which can cultivate compassion within us. We become acutely aware of the emotional toll such reactions can take, prompting us to treat others with kindness and empathy. Failure teaches us the importance of being heard and validated, inspiring us to become better listeners and validators in our relationships.

Failure also teaches us the perils of judgment. We recognize that hastily judging others based on their failures is unfair and unproductive. Instead, we learn to withhold judgment, seek context, and offer support without prejudice.

Empathy enhances communication, allowing us to become more attuned to others' feelings and perspectives. This heightened ability to communicate with empathy and understanding proves invaluable in both personal relationships and professional interactions. Empathetic understanding, cultivated through the lessons of failure, contributes to the strengthening of our relationships. It fosters trust, openness, and emotional connection, enriching our interactions with others.

- Empathy acquired through failure plays a pivotal role in effective teamwork and leadership. Leaders who understand and empathize with their team members can create more inclusive and productive work environments.

- Empathy is also a cornerstone of conflict resolution, enabling us to see disputes from multiple perspectives and find mutually beneficial solutions. This skill is essential in resolving professional conflicts and maintaining harmonious relationships.

- Empathy extends beyond individual relationships to encompass a global perspective. As we learn to empathize with diverse experiences and cultures, we become better global citizens, fostering cooperation and understanding on a broader scale.

In summary, the experience of failure is a profound teacher of empathy. It reminds us of our shared vulnerabilities, encourages compassion, and nurtures our ability to understand and support others. This empathetic understanding, honed through setbacks, enriches both personal and professional relationships, making us more compassionate and effective individuals. As we continue our exploration, we will uncover how these empathetic qualities contribute to building and strengthening meaningful connections in our lives.

How about the transformative power of failure in the context of interpersonal relationships. Failure is not an isolated personal experience but a significant factor influencing how we connect with others, both in our personal lives and our professional endeavors. Let's delve into how setbacks can be harnessed to forge and fortify meaningful connections with the people around us.

One of the profound impacts of failure is its ability to lead us toward vulnerability and authenticity. When we share our failures and setbacks with others, it creates a foundation of trust and openness. Authenticity becomes the bridge to building deeper and more genuine relationships, as individuals connect through shared experiences of resilience and growth.

Empathy, as discussed earlier, is another powerful byproduct of failure. It allows us to better grasp the challenges and emotions experienced by those we interact with. Our heightened empathetic understanding enables us to be more attuned to their needs and concerns, fostering relationships characterized by empathy and support.

Failure teaches us the importance of effective communication, particularly during times of adversity. We learn to express our thoughts, feelings, and concerns more clearly and openly. These improved communication skills not only enhance our ability to connect with others but also equip us to resolve conflicts constructively.

Speaking of conflicts, failure often necessitates navigating them, be they internal or external. Through these experiences, we develop skills in conflict resolution and negotiation. These invaluable skills contribute to maintaining harmonious relationships, both in personal and professional contexts.

The act of sharing our failures and lessons learned creates opportunities for mutual learning. Others can benefit from our experiences, and in turn, we can glean insights from their journeys. This reciprocal learning fosters a sense of collaboration and growth within our relationships.

Failure has the potential to lead to the formation of robust support networks. When we turn to others for guidance and support during challenging times, it strengthens our connections. These networks become pillars of strength in our personal and professional lives, reinforcing the bonds we share with those in our circle.

Our failures also have the power to inspire and empower those around us when we share our stories of overcoming adversity. Such narratives motivate others to persevere in the face of challenges and setbacks. By uplifting and supporting those in our lives, we contribute to building more positive and encouraging relationships.

Failure often arises from diverse perspectives and approaches. Embracing these differences and learning from them can lead to a deeper appreciation for diversity in our relationships. It encourages us to respect varying viewpoints, ultimately enriching our connections with others.

Furthermore, failure can be a shared experience that fosters growth together. When we engage others in our personal growth journeys, it becomes a collective effort. Encouraging personal growth in those we care about strengthens the bonds between us, as we evolve together.

Lastly, failure can instill a profound sense of gratitude and appreciation for the support and relationships in our lives. Expressing gratitude and appreciation deepens the quality of our connections, as it reaffirms the value we place on these vital aspects of our personal and professional worlds.

Harnessing the lessons of failure to build and strengthen relationships is a transformative process. It involves embracing vulnerability, practicing empathy, enhancing communication, resolving conflicts constructively, fostering support networks, empowering others, respecting diverse perspectives, growing together, and expressing gratitude. Failure becomes a catalyst for more meaningful and fulfilling relationships, enriching both our personal and professional lives. As we continue our exploration, we will uncover strategies for leveraging these lessons to nurture lasting connections with those around us.

We now navigate the essential process of reassessing and setting new priorities in the aftermath of failure. Failure often acts as a catalyst for profound self-reflection, and it is during these moments that we have a unique opportunity to realign our priorities, both in our personal lives and our professional endeavors. Let's explore the guidance and strategies for embarking on this crucial journey.

- The Power of Self-Reflection: Failure prompts us to pause and reflect on our goals, values, and aspirations. It offers an opportunity to ask fundamental questions about what truly matters to us. By delving into these introspective moments, we can gain clarity on our priorities moving forward.

- Identifying Lessons Learned: Failure is often accompanied by valuable lessons. We can draw insights from our setbacks to identify what went wrong and why. These lessons can help us reevaluate our priorities with a deeper understanding of our strengths, weaknesses, and areas for improvement.

- Defining Personal Values: Our values are the compass that guides our priorities. After experiencing failure, it's essential to revisit and reaffirm our personal values. What principles and beliefs do we hold dear, and how do they align with our goals? By anchoring our priorities in our values, we create a strong foundation for meaningful progress.

- Balancing Short-Term and Long-Term Goals: Failure can sometimes result from an overemphasis on short-term goals at the expense of long-term vision. Reassessing priorities allows us to strike a healthier balance between immediate objectives and our broader, long-range aspirations.

- Flexibility and Adaptability: Embracing failure requires a willingness to adapt. As we reassess priorities, it's crucial to acknowledge that circumstances change. Our goals and priorities must remain flexible to accommodate unexpected shifts, allowing us to navigate future challenges with resilience.

- Setting Clear and Achievable Goals: After a setback, setting clear, specific, and achievable goals becomes paramount. These goals should align with our revised priorities and provide a roadmap for progress. Breaking them down into manageable steps makes them more attainable.

- Seeking External Guidance: Sometimes, reassessing priorities can benefit from external perspectives. Seeking advice from mentors, coaches, or trusted colleagues can offer fresh insights and guidance as we embark on this transformative journey.

- Adopting a Growth Mindset: Failure can fuel a growth mindset, emphasizing the importance of continuous learning and development. Embracing this mindset enables us to approach our new priorities with enthusiasm, viewing challenges as opportunities for growth.

- Embracing Resilience: Resilience is the bedrock of successful priority reassessment. It allows us to bounce back from failure with renewed determination and adapt to the evolving landscape of our lives and careers.

- Regular Evaluation: Priority reassessment is not a one-time endeavor. It's an ongoing process that should be periodically revisited. Regularly evaluating our priorities ensures that they remain aligned with our evolving goals and values.

The aftermath of failure provides a unique opportunity to reassess and set new priorities. It's a journey of self-discovery, guided by self-reflection, lessons learned, personal values, and a growth mindset. Balancing short-term and long-term goals, seeking external guidance, and maintaining flexibility are key components of this transformative process. Ultimately, reassessing priorities allows us to chart a new course, driven by a clearer sense of purpose and direction. As we delve further into this exploration, we will uncover strategies for translating these reassessed priorities into actionable plans and successful outcomes.

It's essential to maintain balance between our personal and professional lives in the aftermath of failure. Failure can often disrupt this delicate equilibrium, leading to stress and burnout. However, it also presents an opportunity for reevaluating and adjusting our approach to life's demands. Let's explore tips and strategies for ensuring a healthy balance as we move forward.

After experiencing failure, it's essential to prioritize self-care. This includes physical, emotional, and mental well-being. Regular exercise, adequate sleep, and stress management techniques are vital for maintaining balance. Setting clear boundaries between work and personal life is crucial. Define specific work hours and resist the urge to constantly check emails or engage in work-related activities during your personal time.

Effective time management is key to maintaining balance. Create schedules that allocate dedicated time for work, family, and personal pursuits. Use tools and techniques that help you prioritize tasks and stay organized. Focus on the quality of your interactions and efforts, both at work and in your personal life. Being present and fully engaged in the task at hand can lead to greater satisfaction and better results.

Don't hesitate to delegate tasks or seek support when needed, both at work and at home. Surround yourself with a support network that can assist during challenging times. It's important to recognize your limitations and be willing to say no when additional commitments could jeopardize your balance. Setting realistic expectations for yourself is a sign of self-awareness and self-care.

Revisit hobbies and interests that bring you joy and fulfillment. Engaging in activities you are passionate about can help restore balance and provide a sense of purpose beyond work. Mindfulness practices and stress reduction techniques, such as meditation or deep breathing exercises, can help you stay centered and manage stress effectively. If you find it challenging to regain balance on your own, consider seeking professional assistance. A therapist or counselor can provide guidance and strategies for managing stress and maintaining equilibrium.

Reflect on your core values and what truly matters to you. This introspection can guide you in making decisions that align with your priorities and contribute to a balanced life. Open and honest communication with your employer, colleagues, and loved ones is essential. Discuss your needs, boundaries, and expectations to ensure that they understand and support your quest for balance. Periodically assess your work-life balance and make necessary adjustments. Life circumstances change, and what worked previously may need modification as you progress.

Maintaining balance in the wake of failure is a vital aspect of personal and professional well-being. It involves self-care, setting boundaries, effective time management, and a focus on quality rather than quantity. Engaging in activities you love, practicing mindfulness, and seeking support when needed are also essential components of a balanced life. By implementing these strategies, you can not only recover from failure but also thrive in both your personal and professional spheres. As we delve further into this exploration, we will uncover more insights and practical approaches for achieving and sustaining balance.

In this chapter, we've embarked on a journey to explore the multifaceted dimensions of growth that can be achieved through embracing failure. Failure, often seen as a stumbling block, has been revealed as a stepping stone towards holistic development—

nurturing our personal, professional, and emotional growth in profound ways.

Throughout these pages, we've uncovered the transformative power of failure in various aspects of life. We've learned how setbacks can lead to not just resilience, but also to innovation, creativity, and the development of a growth mindset. We've explored how failure deepens our empathy, enhances our relationships, and prompts us to reevaluate our priorities and seek balance.

This chapter has emphasized that failure is not the end of the road but a pivotal moment in our journey. It is a catalyst for self-discovery, pushing us to confront our vulnerabilities and develop the courage to try again. It sparks creativity, encourages adaptability, and fosters empathy—qualities that contribute to our personal and professional success.

The holistic growth achievable through failure is a testament to the human capacity for resilience and adaptation. It reminds us that in the face of adversity, we can emerge stronger, wiser, and more compassionate individuals. By embracing failure as an integral part of our growth story, we open ourselves to a world of possibilities and endless potential.

As we move forward in this book, we will continue to explore the multifaceted nature of failure and the strategies that can transform it into a springboard for success. Our journey is far from over, and the lessons we've learned in this chapter will serve as a foundation for the transformative insights and practical guidance that lie ahead. Embracing failure is not merely a choice; it is a path to holistic growth and enduring resilience.

Chapter 9: Action Plans and Moving Forward

In the ever-evolving world of business, setbacks and failures are not uncommon. Executives, often seen as the captains of their respective ships, are not immune to these challenges. What distinguishes successful leaders is their ability to bounce back and chart a course towards success. This chapter delves into the importance of actionable steps post-failure for executives, emphasizing the need for resilience and adaptability.

Developing Personalized Action Plans

One size does not fit all when it comes to recovery and growth after setbacks. This section explores the art of developing personalized action plans tailored to individual circumstances. By recognizing that each failure is unique, executives can craft strategies that are finely tuned to their specific challenges and goals.

Goal Setting Post-Failure

Setting goals is not merely a routine task but an opportunity to learn from failures. We delve into techniques for effective goal setting, which allows executives to transform their setbacks into valuable lessons. By establishing clear objectives, leaders can navigate the path forward with purpose and clarity.

Strategies for Implementing Action Plans

Crafting a plan is just the beginning; the real test lies in execution. This part of the chapter provides methods to put personalized plans into action. Whether it's aligning teams, utilizing resources efficiently, or overcoming resistance, these strategies will help executives turn their vision into reality.

Monitoring and Adjusting Plans

Progress is seldom linear, and course corrections are often necessary. We explore tools and techniques for tracking progress and making necessary adjustments to action plans. By staying vigilant and flexible, executives can ensure that their strategies remain relevant and effective throughout their journey of recovery and growth.

Learning from Future Failures

Failures are not final; they are stepping stones to success. Preparing to use future setbacks as learning opportunities is a fundamental mindset shift. This section delves into strategies for cultivating a growth-oriented perspective that views failures as valuable experiences.

Resources for Continued Learning

Success is often fueled by knowledge and information. Identifying and accessing resources for ongoing development is crucial. In this part of the chapter, we explore various avenues executives can explore to stay updated and continuously enhance their skillset.

Building a Support Network

No executive is an island. Creating and maintaining a network for support and advice can be a lifeline during challenging times. We discuss the importance of building a support network and provide practical tips for nurturing these relationships.

This chapter serves as a roadmap for executives seeking to navigate the turbulent waters of failure. By understanding the significance of actionable steps, personalized plans, effective goal setting, implementation strategies, monitoring and adjustment, learning from failures, accessing resources, and building a support network, leaders can move forward with confidence and resilience. Success after failure is not only possible but can be a transformative journey filled with growth and valuable insights.

In the world of business, setbacks and failures are inevitable. Even the most accomplished executives can find themselves facing unexpected challenges. However, what truly distinguishes these leaders is their ability to bounce back and set a course for success. This chapter explores the critical importance of taking actionable steps in the aftermath of failure for executives.

Failures can be disheartening, leaving executives feeling adrift and uncertain about the future. Yet, it is precisely in these moments that the need for a structured plan of action becomes apparent. These actionable steps serve as a roadmap for executives, guiding them through the process of recovery and renewal.

One of the key benefits of these steps is their capacity to transform setbacks into valuable learning opportunities. Every failure carries with it a wealth of insights, but these lessons are only realized when they are acted upon. Executives who embark on this journey of recovery through actionable steps are more likely to glean the wisdom that failure has to offer.

Actionable steps also instill a sense of purpose and direction. They help executives set specific objectives and lay out the tasks necessary to achieve them. In doing so, these steps keep leaders firmly grounded in their goals and accountable for their progress.

The ability to adapt is essential in today's ever-changing business landscape. Actionable steps empower executives to remain flexible and responsive to evolving circumstances. By following a structured plan, leaders can adjust their strategies as needed, ensuring their resilience and adaptability.

As leaders within their organizations, executives serve as role models for their teams. By embracing actionable steps post-failure, they demonstrate that setbacks are an integral part of the journey. Their commitment to structured recovery sets an example of resilience and determination, inspiring those they lead.

Beyond personal growth, actionable steps enhance decision-making. Executives who follow these plans are better equipped to evaluate their options, make informed choices, and navigate their organizations toward success.

Stakeholders place great trust in executives. Whether it's employees, investors, or customers, they look to these leaders for guidance and stability. Actionable steps provide assurance that the situation is being managed proactively, which can help maintain stakeholder confidence. Embracing actionable steps fosters a culture of continuous improvement. Executives who view failure as a stepping stone to growth are more inclined to innovate and refine their strategies, leading their organizations toward sustained success.

Actionable steps post-failure are not just a means of recovery; they are a catalyst for growth, resilience, and leadership. They provide a structured framework for executives to transform adversity into opportunity, guiding their organizations to new heights.

The process of crafting personalized action plans is a pivotal endeavor, especially in the aftermath of setbacks. These action plans hold the key to recovery and growth, and they are anything but one-size-fits-all. In times of adversity, executives must recognize that each setback is unique, demanding a tailored response. Developing personalized action plans is a meticulous art that takes into account the specific circumstances and goals of the individual leader.

The essence of this endeavor lies in customization. It involves a thoughtful analysis of what went wrong, the identification of areas that require attention, and the formulation of concrete steps to rectify and improve. It's about dissecting the failure, extracting its core lessons, and using them as building blocks for a brighter future.

Customization goes beyond a simple template or a generic set of actions. It's a deep dive into the executive's strengths, weaknesses, and aspirations. These personalized action plans are not just about recovering lost ground; they're about propelling oneself to new heights.

The art of customization also involves setting the right priorities. Executives must discern what truly matters and allocate their resources and efforts accordingly. It's about investing energy where it will yield the greatest return, ensuring that the action plan is both feasible and impactful.

These personalized action plans are not just about reacting to failure. They are a proactive approach to transformation and renewal. They serve as a compass, guiding the executive through the turbulent waters of recovery, and ultimately, toward a more resilient and prosperous future.

In the wake of failure, the art of setting meaningful and effective goals takes center stage for executives seeking to glean valuable insights from their setbacks. Goal setting, far from being a routine task, becomes a pivotal means of harnessing the lessons that failure offers.

Effective goal setting post-failure hinges on a deliberate and methodical approach. It begins with a profound recognition that setbacks are not merely obstacles to overcome but stepping stones to growth and improvement. In this context, goals are not just targets to achieve; they are waypoints on the journey of transformation.

One technique that emerges as particularly potent in this endeavor is specificity. Executives must be precise in defining their goals. Vague and nebulous objectives only lead to ambiguity and frustration. Instead, setting concrete, measurable, and achievable goals is paramount. By doing so, executives gain clarity and direction in their pursuit of post-failure growth.

Effective goal setting entails a comprehensive understanding of the root causes of failure. It requires executives to dig deep, dissecting the failure to identify its core components. This insight becomes the bedrock upon which meaningful goals are constructed.

Another critical technique is alignment. Goals should be aligned with the lessons learned from failure. They should directly address the weaknesses or shortcomings that contributed to the setback. By doing this, executives ensure that their goals are not just arbitrary aspirations but strategic responses to their unique circumstances.

Furthermore, flexibility is an essential aspect of post-failure goal setting. Executives must be open to adjusting their goals as they progress. This adaptability allows them to remain responsive to changing conditions and evolving insights. It's a recognition that the path to recovery and growth is rarely a straight line. The process of goal setting post-failure is not an isolated event. It's an ongoing, iterative process that unfolds in tandem with the executive's journey of transformation. It's about using the canvas of failure as a backdrop for painting a picture of success. In this context, goals serve as the brushstrokes that gradually reveal the masterpiece of resilience and achievement.

In the realm of executive leadership, the importance of strategies for effectively implementing personalized action plans cannot be overstated, particularly in the context of post-failure recovery and growth. Crafting these intricate plans is only the first step; it's the execution that truly matters. Implementing action plans requires a deliberate and methodical approach, one that bridges the gap between intention and achievement. Executives must translate their well-crafted plans into tangible results. Here, we delve into the methods that empower leaders to breathe life into their personalized strategies.

One key method we mentioned involves alignment. Executives must ensure that the actions they take are in perfect harmony with the objectives outlined in their personalized plans. Alignment is the compass that guides every decision and effort, ensuring that they contribute directly to the overarching goal. Effective implementation hinges on resource allocation. Executives need to allocate their resources, whether it's time, finances, or manpower, judiciously. Resource management is about prioritizing activities that will yield the greatest impact and optimizing the use of available assets.

Effective communication also emerges as a vital strategy. Executives must articulate their plans and objectives clearly to their teams, fostering understanding and buy-in. In turn, this enhances collaboration and empowers employees to contribute meaningfully to the plan's execution. Overcoming resistance is another facet of implementation strategies. Change often meets resistance, and executives must be prepared to address it. This involves identifying potential barriers, whether they are internal or external, and devising tactics to navigate them.

Monitoring progress is an ongoing strategy that ensures that actions are aligned with the plan and producing the desired results. By regularly assessing how well the plan is being executed and the impact it is having, executives can make timely adjustments to stay on course. Perseverance is a cornerstone of successful implementation. Executives must remain steadfast in their commitment to seeing the plan through, even when faced with challenges and setbacks. A resilient and determined approach is often the difference between success and stagnation.

Strategies for implementing action plans are the bridge that connects vision to reality. They are the engine that propels executives and their organizations from planning to achievement, transforming personalized plans into concrete results and, ultimately, fostering resilience and growth.

In the dynamic landscape of executive leadership, the ability to effectively monitor and adjust plans stands as a cornerstone of success, particularly in the context of post-failure recovery and growth. A well-crafted plan is not set in stone but rather a flexible roadmap that evolves with changing circumstances.

Monitoring progress is the first essential component of this process. It involves the diligent and systematic tracking of how well the plan is being executed and whether it is yielding the anticipated results. Executives must deploy a range of tools and metrics to keep a finger on the pulse of their strategies.

These tools serve as a lens through which executives can gain insights into the plan's performance. Metrics, key performance indicators (KPIs), and regular check-ins provide a real-time snapshot of progress. This enables leaders to identify areas of strength, acknowledge successes, and, perhaps most importantly, pinpoint areas that require adjustment.

Adjusting plans is the natural next step once insights have been gathered through monitoring. It is a dynamic and adaptive approach that acknowledges the fluidity of the business environment. Executives must be ready to recalibrate their strategies based on the data and feedback received.

This adjustment process is not an admission of failure but rather a testament to adaptability and strategic acumen. It is a proactive response to changing conditions and a commitment to ensuring that the plan remains relevant and effective.

Crucially, this approach involves a willingness to revisit the goals and objectives set initially. It may entail modifying timelines, reallocating resources, or even revising the strategy altogether. The ability to make these decisions thoughtfully and decisively is a hallmark of effective leadership. Executives must communicate these adjustments transparently to their teams and stakeholders. Transparency fosters trust and alignment, ensuring that everyone is on the same page and committed to the revised path forward.

Monitoring and adjusting plans is not an optional exercise but a fundamental aspect of executive leadership. It's about staying agile and responsive in a rapidly changing world. It's about transforming setbacks into opportunities and ensuring that the journey toward recovery and growth remains on course.

In the ever-evolving landscape of executive leadership, there exists a profound wisdom in preparing to glean valuable lessons from future failures. It is a forward-thinking approach that recognizes that setbacks are not final destinations but rather stepping stones to growth and development.

Learning from future failures entails a fundamental shift in mindset. It's about embracing a perspective that reframes failures as valuable experiences. Rather than shying away from adversity, executives who adopt this mindset actively seek out opportunities to learn and grow.

One crucial aspect of this approach is reflection. Executives must take the time to analyze the root causes of failures, dissecting them to uncover underlying issues. This introspection is not an exercise in blame but an exploration of the factors that contributed to the setback. Learning from future failures requires a commitment to continuous improvement. Executives must be willing to adapt and evolve, integrating the insights gained from each setback into their leadership repertoire. This iterative process ensures that mistakes are not repeated but instead become catalysts for progress.

It's also vital to recognize that learning from future failures extends beyond individual growth. It can profoundly impact organizational culture. Executives who model a growth-oriented approach to setbacks inspire their teams to do the same. This creates a culture of resilience and adaptability within the organization.

Executives should be proactive in seeking feedback and diverse perspectives. Learning from future failures is not a solitary endeavor but a collaborative one. By soliciting input from others and considering alternative viewpoints, leaders can gain a more comprehensive understanding of what went wrong and how to improve.

It's essential to approach future failures with a sense of curiosity and humility. This mindset acknowledges that no one is infallible, and failures are a natural part of the journey. Embracing them as opportunities for growth rather than sources of shame or fear fosters a culture of innovation and resilience.

Learning from future failures is a profound and forward-looking approach to executive leadership. It's about turning adversity into an asset, using setbacks as stepping stones toward personal and organizational growth. Executives who adopt this mindset are better equipped to navigate the complexities of the business world and emerge stronger with each challenge they encounter.

In the realm of executive leadership, the pursuit of continuous learning is a hallmark of success. Executives must not only acknowledge the ever-evolving nature of business but actively seek out resources that enable their ongoing development. Identifying and accessing resources for continued learning is a strategic endeavor that empowers leaders to stay at the forefront of their field. In a world where knowledge is a dynamic currency, executives must be vigilant in expanding their intellectual capital.

One critical aspect of this pursuit is resource identification. Executives must have a discerning eye for recognizing valuable sources of knowledge and insights. These resources can take various forms, including books, articles, seminars, workshops, industry conferences, and online courses. Resource identification extends beyond traditional sources. It also encompasses networking and mentorship opportunities. Engaging with peers and seeking guidance from experienced mentors can provide a wealth of knowledge and wisdom.

Once identified, executives must actively access these resources. This involves a commitment to setting aside time for learning and personal development. It requires discipline and a willingness to invest in one's own growth. Furthermore, executives should be open to exploring a diverse range of resources. The business landscape is multifaceted, and insights can be found in unexpected places. Reading outside one's industry, engaging with experts from various fields, and considering unconventional perspectives can yield fresh insights and innovative ideas.

Executives should leverage technology to access resources conveniently. The digital age has made a wealth of knowledge easily accessible through online platforms, webinars, and elearning courses. Embracing these technological resources can enhance the efficiency of continuous learning.

Resources for continued learning are the lifeblood of executive growth and adaptability. They are the foundation upon which informed decisions, strategic innovation, and professional development are built. Executives who prioritize and actively engage with these resources are not only better equipped to lead but also poised to thrive in an ever-changing business landscape.

In the realm of executive leadership, the significance of building a robust support network is essential. Building a support network is akin to constructing a safety net in the challenging landscape of executive leadership. It is a deliberate and strategic endeavor that offers numerous advantages, particularly during times of adversity and uncertainty.

The process begins with the identification of individuals and resources that can serve as pillars of support. These may include mentors, peers, industry experts, or even professional organizations. The key is to seek out individuals who can offer guidance, insights, and a fresh perspective on the challenges faced.

Building a support network involves proactively cultivating these relationships. It's not enough to merely connect with individuals; ongoing engagement is essential. This entails regular communication, seeking advice, and providing assistance in return. Reciprocity is at the heart of a thriving support network.

A well-rounded network also spans both personal and professional spheres. Executives should not limit themselves to a single type of connection. Personal relationships, such as friends and family, can provide emotional support and a sense of balance that is invaluable in high-stress roles.

Executives must be attuned to the changing dynamics of their network. It's essential to assess the evolving needs and challenges and adjust the network accordingly. This adaptability ensures that the support received remains relevant and effective.

Building a support network is not a one-time endeavor but an ongoing process. It requires patience, effort, and a genuine interest in the well-being of those within the network. In turn, it provides executives with a safety net that can buoy them during challenging times and offer guidance during critical decisions. Creating and maintaining a support network is a strategic imperative for executives. It's about recognizing that no one can navigate the complexities of leadership in isolation. A robust support network is the cornerstone of resilience, offering a lifeline of advice, perspective, and emotional sustenance throughout one's professional journey.

As we conclude this chapter, it's essential to distill the key takeaways that encapsulate the essence of moving forward after failure in the realm of executive leadership. These insights serve as a compass, guiding executives on a path towards recovery, growth, and lasting success.

First and foremost, it is imperative to understand that setbacks are not the end but a part of the journey. Executives must embrace failure as a stepping stone to growth, a crucible of learning, and an opportunity to become more resilient leaders. The importance of actionable steps post-failure cannot be overstated. A well-thought-out plan, customized to one's unique circumstances, is the foundation of recovery. It provides clarity, direction, and a sense of purpose in the face of adversity.

Goal setting post-failure is not a mere formality but a deliberate act of learning. Specific, measurable, and aligned goals serve as beacons, guiding executives toward a brighter future and helping them avoid the pitfalls of the past. Implementing action plans is where the rubber meets the road. Alignment, resource allocation, communication, and perseverance are the strategies that transform plans into reality. Effective execution is the linchpin of success.

Monitoring and adjusting plans are the twin engines that ensure that strategies remain on track. Regular assessment and adaptation are vital to staying responsive to changing conditions and evolving insights. Learning from future failures is a mindset shift that views setbacks as opportunities. Reflection, continuous improvement, feedback, and curiosity are the tools that turn failures into catalysts for personal and organizational growth.

Resources for continued learning are the wellspring of knowledge and innovation. Identifying and accessing these resources ensures that executives remain at the forefront of their fields, equipped with the latest insights and expertise. Building a support network is the safety net that executives can rely on during challenging times. It provides guidance, advice, and emotional support, fostering resilience and balance in the high-stakes world of leadership.

Moving forward after failure is a journey that demands resilience, adaptability, and a commitment to growth. These key takeaways serve as a roadmap, helping executives navigate the complex terrain of executive leadership with confidence and purpose. Success is not only possible but can be a transformative journey filled with growth and valuable insights.

Conclusion

In "Embracing Setbacks," we have explored the transformative power of failure in the business and leadership arenas. We challenged the stigma surrounding setbacks, arguing for their essential role in fostering innovation and resilience. Throughout this book, our aim was to shift the mindset from fearing failure to leveraging it as a catalyst for growth. We delved into the creation of a supportive organizational culture that views mistakes as learning opportunities, emphasizing the leader's role in cultivating such an environment. We shared practical strategies and real-world examples to guide leaders in implementing these principles, fostering a culture where risk-taking and learning from failure are celebrated.

Our discussion extended to key concepts like reflective practice and the significance of psychological safety in teams, offering insights on how to build resilience and encourage open sharing of setbacks. We provided tools for executives to apply these concepts, creating an environment that nurtures innovation and team cohesion. We also touched upon personal growth through navigating failures, advocating for vulnerability in leadership. We suggest embracing one's own setbacks as opportunities for profound professional development and a more authentic leadership style, encouraging leaders to lead by example.

We conclude by urging leaders to embrace a paradigm shift towards viewing setbacks as opportunities. "Embracing Setbacks" is a call to action for leaders to foster adaptability, openness, and continuous improvement, creating a legacy of innovation, resilience, and success within their organizations.

We have explored the untapped potential that lies within the experiences of failure, urging readers to reframe their perspective on setbacks as opportunities for growth and innovation. We began by dismantling the stigma associated with failure, arguing that it is not a mark of defeat but rather a stepping stone towards greater achievements. By embracing failure, individuals and organizations can unlock a deeper understanding of their capabilities, limitations, and the paths to overcoming them.

We delved into the concept of failure as a catalyst for innovation, highlighting how history's most groundbreaking discoveries often emerged from the ashes of apparent defeats. Through engaging narratives, we illustrated the resilience of leaders and teams who have harnessed the lessons from their failures to fuel creative solutions and strategic pivots. This part of the narrative emphasized the importance of fostering an environment where experimentation and learning from mistakes are encouraged, thereby cultivating a culture of agility and continuous improvement.

The narrative further explored the psychological aspects of dealing with failure, offering insights into how individuals can develop resilience. We introduced strategies for cultivating a growth mindset, a crucial element for seeing beyond the immediate setback and recognizing the potential for personal and professional development. By shifting focus from the fear of failing to the learning opportunities it presents, individuals can build a more resilient and adaptive approach to challenges.

Again, this is a call to action for leaders, teams, and individuals to embrace and learn from their setbacks. We argue that by doing so, they not only enhance their own capacity for innovation and growth but also contribute to a more resilient, adaptable, and forward-thinking organizational culture. The book serves as a guide for transforming the way we perceive and respond to failure, positioning it as a powerful tool for achieving success in an ever-changing world.

We chronicled the pivotal role of adaptability in navigating setbacks, offering readers a blueprint for thriving in an ever-evolving landscape. We began by illustrating the relentless pace of change in the modern business world, highlighting that adaptability is not merely beneficial but essential for survival and success. Through stories of companies and leaders who faced significant disruptions, we demonstrated how those who embraced adaptability turned potential crises into opportunities for growth and innovation.

We delved into the mechanisms of adaptability, revealing it as a multifaceted skill that encompasses the ability to anticipate changes, the flexibility to adjust strategies, and the resilience to overcome challenges. By drawing on research and case studies, we showed that adaptability fuels problem-solving and creative thinking, enabling individuals and organizations to navigate the complexities of change with confidence.

The narrative also addressed the psychological and cultural dimensions of adaptability, emphasizing the importance of cultivating a mindset that views change as an opportunity rather than a threat. We offered practical advice on building this mindset at both the individual and organizational levels, suggesting ways to foster an environment that encourages experimentation, learning, and the continuous reassessment of goals and strategies in response to new information.

We have affirmed that adaptability is a critical determinant of long-term success. We urged leaders and individuals alike to embrace the inevitability of change, viewing each setback as a stepping stone towards greater achievements. Through adaptability, we posited, businesses and professionals can not only withstand the winds of change but also harness them to sail towards uncharted territories of opportunity and growth.

We examined how leaders can steer their teams through setbacks and transform failures into opportunities for growth. The narrative began by underscoring the inevitability of failure in the pursuit of innovation and success. Leaders, we argued, play a crucial role in shaping their team's response to these setbacks, turning potentially demoralizing experiences into valuable learning moments.

The book then delved into the strategies leaders can employ to foster a culture of resilience and adaptability. By embracing transparency, encouraging open dialogue about failures, and demonstrating vulnerability, leaders can destigmatize failure within their organizations. This approach not only strengthens the collective resolve to overcome challenges but also cultivates an environment where creativity and innovation are nurtured.

We explored the importance of reflective leadership—how leaders can learn from their own mistakes and model this behavior for their teams. Through personal anecdotes and case studies, we illustrated the transformative power of leaders who actively reflect on their failures, extract lessons, and apply this knowledge to future challenges. This reflective practice was presented as essential for personal growth and the continuous improvement of the team and organization.

Furthermore, we emphasized that learning from failure was an ongoing journey, not a destination. The book championed the idea that leaders who were committed to personal and organizational growth, who approached setbacks with curiosity and resilience, were best positioned to navigate the complexities of the modern business world. By embodying these principles, leaders inspired their teams to embrace challenges, learn from their missteps, and ultimately, drive their organizations toward greater innovation and success.

Building resilient organizations involved creating an environment where teams and companies were not only prepared to face challenges but could also thrive in the aftermath. It started with fostering a culture that valued adaptability, open communication, and mutual support among its members. Leaders played a critical role in this process by setting an example of resilience, encouraging learning from failures, and providing the resources and support necessary for individuals and teams to bounce back from setbacks.

Strategies for enhancing resilience included implementing robust planning and risk management practices to anticipate and mitigate potential impacts of adverse events. Encouraging collaboration and cross-functional team support also strengthened the network within the organization, ensuring a collective capacity to respond to challenges. Investing in training and development programs that focused on resilience skills, such as problem-solving, emotional intelligence, and stress management, equipped employees with the tools they needed to navigate difficulties more effectively.

An essential element of building resilient organizations was the creation of a supportive and inclusive workplace culture. This involved recognizing and valuing diversity, ensuring equity in opportunities and resources, and fostering a sense of belonging among all employees. Such a culture not only enhanced team cohesion but also improved the organization's ability to innovate and adapt to change.

Building resilient organizations required a holistic approach that encompassed leadership, culture, planning, and personal development. By prioritizing resilience, companies could not only withstand the challenges they faced but also emerge stronger, more agile, and better positioned for future success. This resilience became a competitive advantage, enabling organizations to thrive in an increasingly complex and unpredictable business landscape.

The narrative highlighted the importance of clear communication, continuous learning, and strategic planning as foundational tools for success. It underscored the significance of developing a growth mindset, encouraging innovation, and maintaining a focus on long-term goals even in the face of setbacks. Practical advice on creating supportive environments where feedback is welcomed and failures are viewed as learning experiences helps to cultivate a culture of continuous improvement.

We provided guidelines for applying ethical principles in decision-making, ensuring that actions taken in response to failure or change are aligned with the organization's core values. suggests mechanisms for fostering ethical behavior and accountability, reinforcing the idea that integrity should never be compromised for short-term gains. By adopting these practices, leaders can build more resilient, ethical, and adaptable organizations capable of thriving in an ever-changing business landscape.

Encouraging continuous learning is about instilling a mindset that values growth, curiosity, and the pursuit of knowledge as lifelong endeavors. This section emphasized the importance of continuous learning as a key driver of personal development and organizational success. It argued that in a rapidly changing world, the ability to adapt and grow is essential, and continuous learning is the mechanism that enables this adaptability.

We explored strategies for fostering a learning culture within organizations, including creating opportunities for education, encouraging mentorship, and rewarding curiosity and innovation. The narrative highlighted the benefits of continuous learning, not just for individual career advancement but also for enhancing team collaboration and driving the organization forward. By investing in the development of their people, leaders can build a more knowledgeable, agile, and resilient workforce. The narrative also addressed the challenges to continuous learning, such as time constraints and the fear of failure, and offers practical solutions to overcome these barriers. We underscored the role of technology in facilitating accessible and flexible learning opportunities, making it easier for individuals to integrate learning into their daily lives.

As we gaze into the future, the evolving business landscape suggests that failure will play an increasingly central role in fostering innovation and driving growth. This shift acknowledges that failure is not just an inevitable part of business but a valuable source of insight and learning. Organizations that integrate this understanding into their culture and operations are poised to navigate the complexities of the market with greater agility and resilience.

The ability to rapidly learn from setbacks and adapt strategies accordingly will become a hallmark of competitive advantage. As businesses face unprecedented challenges, from technological disruptions to shifting consumer preferences, the lessons gleaned from failures will be critical in steering these organizations towards success. This necessitates a proactive approach to failure, where businesses actively seek out and analyze their setbacks to extract actionable learnings.

The role of leadership in this context cannot be overstated. Leaders who champion a mindset that views failure as an opportunity will cultivate an organizational ethos that encourages experimentation, risk-taking, and continuous improvement. This leadership approach will be instrumental in building teams that are not only resilient but also innovative and forward-thinking.

The integration of technology in analyzing failures will also be a significant trend. Advanced analytics, artificial intelligence, and machine learning will offer deeper insights into failures, enabling more nuanced understanding and strategic planning. These technologies will assist in predicting potential pitfalls and optimizing decision-making processes, further embedding the value of learning from failure into the organizational DNA.

The future business environment demands an embrace of failure as a pivotal element of strategy. This perspective will drive the development of more adaptable, innovative, and resilient organizations, ready to thrive in an ever-changing global market. The shift towards viewing failure as a vital learning tool reflects a broader evolution towards a more dynamic, agile approach to business strategy and leadership.

As we draw our exploration to a close, we reflect on the profound insights and transformative potential that embracing setbacks offers. This journey underscores that setbacks are not merely obstacles but essential elements of the growth process. They are the crucibles within which resilience is forged and from which innovation springs. Embracing this perspective shifts the narrative of failure from one of defeat to a narrative of opportunity and learning.

The chapters within have not only provided strategies and insights but have also sought to instill a deeper understanding of the intrinsic value found in facing and learning from failures. It's through these moments of setback that we are given the opportunity to reassess, to refine, and to emerge stronger, equipped with newfound knowledge and perspectives. This process is fundamental to personal development and organizational advancement, laying the groundwork for future successes.

The role of leadership in fostering a culture that celebrates learning from setbacks cannot be overstated. Leaders have the unique capability to transform the perception of failure within their organizations, promoting a culture where every challenge is viewed as a stepping stone to greater achievements. This leadership approach is pivotal in cultivating an environment where innovation thrives, and resilience is built.

The journey towards embracing setbacks is continuous, an ever-evolving process that enriches both the individual and the collective. It requires persistence, courage, and an unwavering commitment to growth. As we conclude, let this narrative serve not just as a guide but as a source of inspiration. May it encourage you to navigate your path with resilience, to view setbacks not as termini but as gateways to discovery and innovation, and to embrace the boundless opportunities that lie in every moment of challenge.

As we part ways, remember that the journey of learning from failure is infinite, filled with endless possibilities for those brave enough to embark on it. Embrace each setback with an open heart and mind, ready to uncover the lessons and opportunities they present. Let this mindset of resilience, curiosity, and relentless pursuit of growth guide you towards a future where every failure is a milestone of success, every challenge a catalyst for innovation, and every setback a testament to your strength and perseverance.

www.ingramcontent.com/pod-product-compliance
Lightning Source LLC
Chambersburg PA
CBHW070914290526
45795CB00001B/317